Gregg
Dictation
Simplified

LOUIS A. LESLIE

CHARLES E. ZOUBEK

MADELINE S. STRONY

shorthand written by **CHARLES RADER**

Gregg Publishing Division

McGraw-Hill Book Company, Inc.

NEW YORK   CHICAGO   SAN FRANCISCO

DALLAS   TORONTO   LONDON

GREGG

Dictation

Simplified

SECOND EDITION

Feb. 1960-RD-13

PUBLISHED BY GREGG PUBLISHING DIVISION
McGraw-Hill Book Company, Inc.
Printed in the United States of America

Acknowledgments

The authors wish to acknowledge the valuable help that they received from shorthand teachers in various parts of the country. Special acknowledgment is due Mr. Charles Rader for writing the beautiful shorthand in this book. The authors are also indebted to Mr. Robert Sutter, designer, who contributed so much to the attractiveness of the book.

PREFACE

Gregg Dictation Simplified has been a popular and vitally important part of the program of Gregg Shorthand Simplified materials since they were first published in 1949. Designed to follow *Gregg Shorthand Manual Simplified* or *Gregg Shorthand Manual Simplified, Functional Method*, this book serves as the link between shorthand theory and advanced dictation. For some students, it also serves as the terminal course in shorthand. Specifically, it is designed to help the student achieve four major objectives:

1. To review and strengthen his knowledge of the system.
2. To develop his power to construct new outlines rapidly from dictation.
3. To extend his knowledge and skill in the basic elements of transcription.
4. To lay a solid foundation for further development of dictation and transcription skill.

This Second Edition contains several outstanding new features, many of which are based on suggestions given by teachers who have used the initial edition.

Emphasis on Transcription

Perhaps the most significant new feature is the closer and earlier coordination in the shorthand course of transcription training along with the development of skill in shorthand.

The emphasis on transcription in this edition is carried out through the following features:

Marginal Reminders. Chapters 1 and 2 review the transcription points that are introduced in the *Gregg Shorthand Manual Simplified*, Second Edition. Seven new transcription points are presented in Chapters 3 and 4.

The punctuation marks and marginal reminders appear in color. Through this use of color, these important reminders are high-lighted for the student, so that he cannot miss them.

Transcription Word Studies. In *Gregg Dictation Simplified*, Second Edition, the Transcription Word Studies help to build the student's vocabulary and to distinguish between words that might be confusing in transcribing. Thus, the Transcription Word Studies take two forms:

1. In Chapters 1 through 4—similar words that stenographers often confuse. Each lesson contains a pair or group of similar words, which are defined and illustrated. These words are then used several times in the Reading and Writing Practice of the lesson.

2. In Chapters 5 through 16—definitions of words that may be unfamiliar to the student. These words are selected from the Reading and Writing Practice exercises of the lesson.

Transcription Quizzes. These "quizzes" give the student practice in supplying commas and semicolons in the shorthand material, as well as words that have been omitted. Because he must face this type of transcription problem on the job, these quizzes are valuable transcription-training devices.

Office-Style Dictation. In Chapters 13 through 16, four of the simplest problems of office-style dictation are introduced. Each problem is explained and then illustrated in a letter that is written in shorthand. This feature will be especially valuable to those students whose shorthand training will end with *Gregg Dictation Simplified.*

Recall Drills

Each chapter contains a cycle of drills designed to provide a quick, intensive recall of important elements of Gregg Shorthand. Many of the words and phrases that appear in these drills are woven into the Reading and Writing Practice exercises of the lesson. This cycle includes:

Phrase Builders. The first lesson in each chapter contains a list of commonly used business-letter phrases. The selection of phrases is based on an analysis of more than 250,000 words of business-letter material. Each Phrase Builder is followed by a specially constructed phrase letter, which contains a number of the phrases in the drill. This letter is used for warmup purposes throughout the chapter.

Brief-Form Charts. The second lesson in each chapter contains a chart of brief forms. These charts not only give the student a quick recall of the primitive forms, but, even more important, give him beneficial practice on derivatives.

Geographical Expressions. The second lesson in each chapter also contains a drill on geographical expressions. Many of these geographical expressions are used in the Reading and Writing Practice of the lesson.

Word Families. The third lesson in each chapter contains a group of four word families. These word families enable the student to take the fullest advantage of analogy in outline construction. Because each word in a family group has a common beginning or ending, the student can learn the entire group easily and quickly.

Word Beginnings and Endings. The fourth lesson in each chapter contains an intensive review of several word beginnings and endings. Through these drills, the student reviews intensively each word beginning and ending of the system at least once; the more important ones, several times.

Vocabulary Builders. The fifth lesson in each chapter contains a vocabulary builder that reviews intensively the major word-building features of the system, such as blends, omission of vowels, numbers and quantities, etc.

Connected Practice Material

In building shorthand speed and accuracy, it is essential that the student read and copy a great deal of well-written shorthand. In *Gregg Dictation Simplified,* Second Edition, the student has a wealth of shorthand material in the form of business letters and articles

In order to give the student the dictation "flavor" of many kinds of businesses, each of the sixteen chapters in the book is devoted to correspondence relating to a specific business or department of a business. Each chapter opens with a brief discussion, attractively illustrated, of the business or department that is the subject of the chapter. The letters in the practice material are easy and short.

Secretarial Training

A unique feature of this Second Edition is the use of Secretarial Pointers in the last lesson of each chapter. In these "pointers," actual case studies have been used to emphasize the importance of some of the desirable traits or characteristics of a good secretary, secretarial procedures, and so on. To make these pointers really meaningful, the student is given several questions to answer that test his comprehension of the subject matter.

Gregg Dictation Simplified, Second Edition, has been prepared with the student and teacher in mind. Many teachers and shorthand specialists offered valuable suggestions and guidance in the preparation of this revision. The authors hope that they—and teachers everywhere—will be pleased with the result.

The Publishers

PART ONE

Your Speed-Building Program

AT THE TIME YOU completed the *Gregg Shorthand Manual Simplified*, you also took a big step in the direction of becoming a stenographer or a secretary. Here are some of the things you accomplished:

You learned the alphabet of Gregg Shorthand and so have the means with which to form a shorthand outline for any word in the English language.

You learned many useful abbreviating devices such as brief forms, word beginnings and endings, and phrases that will help you write shorthand rapidly.

You gave attention to three important factors that will help you become a good transcriber—(1) vocabulary, (2) spelling, and (3) punctuation.

In short, you built a fine foundation for the task ahead — developing your ability to take dictation easily and transcribe accurately on the typewriter. You will find this one of the most interesting phases of your shorthand study. You will experience the thrill of watching your shorthand speed grow and your ability to handle words and to punctuate improve almost from day to day.

Your study program at this point will be divided into two major parts — what you do at home and what you do in class.

AT HOME

At home you will read many letters and articles from shorthand and copy them. This should be a simple and pleasant task for you, as there will be no new shorthand devices to learn. This reading and copying will provide an almost daily review of the principles of Gregg Shorthand. At the same time it will stock your mind with the joinings of the shorthand strokes, so that you will be able to recall and write them rapidly when you take dictation.

As you read and copy this shorthand material, you will also continue to improve in your ability to spell and to punctuate.

At home, you will also work with special word drills, word studies, and other interesting devices that will add further to your skill.

YOUR PRACTICE PROCEDURES

To be sure that you practice correctly at home and get the greatest benefit from the time you invest, let us review briefly the procedures you should follow:

1. Always *read* all shorthand before you copy it. Read aloud if possible.

2. When you come to an outline you cannot read, *spell* it. If the spelling does not give you the outline, write it on a slip of paper and find out its meaning in class the next day. Do not spend more than a few seconds trying to decipher any outline. At this stage, there will not be many outlines that you cannot read.

3. After reading the material, make a shorthand copy, reading aloud to yourself as you write. Write as rapidly as you can. Be sure, however, that you write readable shorthand.

IN CLASS

In class, most of your time will be devoted to taking dictation at constantly increasing speeds. Your teacher will see to it that you get the right kind of dictation at the proper speeds so that your dictation skill will increase steadily and rapidly.

CHAPTER One

Credits and Collections

A very large part of today's business is done on a credit basis. Your father may purchase a new car and pay for it in monthly installments. Your mother may purchase a new coat or dress and pay for it perhaps 30 days later. A business organization may purchase goods, equipment, and services "on account" and pay for them in the future.

Most people make their payments when they are due — as they should. Occasionally, however, some do not. Some just forget, and a brief reminder is all they need. Others discover that they are short of funds, for one reason or another, when their bills become due; and, consequently, they cannot pay. Special payment terms often have to be arranged for these people. Still others — only a small minority — make no effort to pay, even though they have the money. These often have to be threatened with legal action before they will pay.

The person whose job it is to see that customers who have been granted credit pay their bills is the credit manager. His job is an important one indeed; for, in addition to collecting the money, he must guard against creating ill will. If he succeeds in collecting an overdue account but loses the customer in the process, he has hurt rather than helped his company.

As most collections must be handled by mail, you can see the important part that collection letters play in the success of a business.

The letters in this chapter contain some simple reminders, some follow-up letters, and a few "get tough" letters. If you were a secretary to a credit manager of an organization, these are the types of letters you would take from dictation.

As you learned in the *Gregg Shorthand Manual Simplified*, a stenographer or a secretary must be able to do more than take shorthand rapidly and accurately; he must be able to spell and punctuate correctly if he is to turn out letters that the employer will have no hesitation in signing. In the *Gregg Shorthand Manual Simplified*, you studied a number of the simpler uses of the comma as they occurred in the Reading and Writing Practice. You also gave attention to those words that stenographers and secretaries often misspell.

In *Gregg Dictation Simplified*, you will take up a number of new and more advanced points of punctuation as well as continue your efforts to become a good speller.

Before you are introduced to these new points, however, you will brush up on those that you studied in the *Gregg Shorthand Manual Simplified*. In Chapter 1 of *Gregg Dictation Simplified*, you will review four uses of the comma; and in Chapter 2 you will complete the review.

To be sure that you have not forgotten how to handle the punctuation and spelling treated in the marginal reminders of the Reading and Writing Practice, let us review briefly the procedure you should use:

1. Read carefully the explanations and illustrative examples of the marginal reminders that follow these explanations.

2. Each time you meet a comma as you read the Reading and Writing Practice, glance in the left margin of the page to be sure that you know the reason why the comma was used.

3. As you copy the Reading and Writing Practice, insert each comma in your shorthand notes and encircle it.

4. Spell all words in the marginal reminders once, preferably aloud.

, parenthetical

A writer will sometimes insert in a sentence a comment or explanation that could be omitted without changing the meaning of the sentence. These added comments or explanations are parenthetical and are separated from the rest of the sentence by commas.

> We shall be glad, however, to cancel the bill.
> Won't you take a few minutes to write us, Mr. Smith.

, apposition

Sometimes a writer mentions a person or a thing and then, in order to make his meaning perfectly clear, says the same thing in different words. This added explanation is known as an expression "in apposition." An expression in apposition is set off by two commas, except when it occurs at the end of the sentence, in which case only one comma is necessary.

> Our credit manager, Mr. Brown, sent you three letters.
> Please see Mr. Gray, the personnel manager.

, series

When three or more similar expressions (words, phrases, or clauses) occur in a series with a conjunction before the last expression, a comma should be placed before the conjunction as well as between the items.

> We wrote you on March 10, April 15, and May 11.
> Your action can result in a wrong impression, in a misunderstanding, or in loss of confidence.

, conjunction

A comma is used to separate two independent clauses that are joined by a conjunction.

> Send us your check, or at least give us an explanation.
> I know you have been busy, but haven't we all?

Hyphenated before noun
No noun, no hyphen

You can quickly determine whether to use a hyphen in expressions such as *worth while* and *past due* by observing these two simple rules:

If a noun follows the expression, use a hyphen; if no noun follows the expression, no hyphen is used.

> Your account is *past due*. (No noun after the expression.)
> Your *past-due* account needs attention. (Noun follows the expression.)

1. Phrase Builder. The following list contains 50 phrases that are frequently used in business letters. Can you read the entire list in 1 minute?

Of the, in the, Yours truly, to the, Dear Mr., we are, Dear Sir, for the.
Yours very truly, on the, it is, we have, will be, of our, that the, with the,
   Very truly yours.
I am, and the, at the, to be, of this, you can, I have, you have, you are.
By the, to make, from the, there is, in our, more than, is the, to our.
That is, we can, in this, to have, to get, so that, of course, they are.
There are, have been, to see, we shall, to us, you may, about the, we will.

▶ **Warmup Phrase Letter.** The following 120-word letter, which is your warmup for this chapter, contains 33 frequently used phrases. After you have read the letter, do you think that you could copy it in 2 minutes?

2.

(120)

Reading and Writing Practice

3. Transcription Word Study. The efficient stenographer or secretary has a good command of words. In these Transcription Word Studies you will continue to build your knowledge and understanding of words. Be sure to read each Transcription Word Study carefully before you tackle the Reading and Writing Practice.

Two words that are often confused because they sound alike are *past* and *passed*.

> **past** (*noun*) Time gone by. (*Past* is also used as an adjective.)

> We received many orders from you in the past.
> His account was past due.

passed   Moved along, went by, transferred.

He passed him on the street.
Before many days had passed, he paid the money.
I passed the sugar to the man next to me.

These two words are used a number of times in the letters of this lesson. Be sure that you select the correct word each time.

4.

, apposition
past due

no noun,
no hyphen

passed
, conjunction

, conjunction
, parenthetical

(98)

15

5.

, apposition
yours

occur
, parenthetical

, conjunction

(138)

6.

past-due
  hyphenated
  before noun
, series

16

, conjunction
arrangements
balance

(58)

7.

Thursday
, apposition

, parenthetical
, conjunction
receive

won't
, parenthetical

(81)

Transcription Quiz. You are already familiar with this type of quiz from your work with the *Gregg Shorthand Manual Simplified*. This quiz gives you an opportunity to see how well you can punctuate and whether you can supply from the meaning of the sentence words that have been omitted from the shorthand. In Chapters 1 and 2 of this book, the Transcription Quiz will contain the same type of problems as those in the *Gregg Shorthand Manual Simplified*. In later chapters, as new points of punctuation are introduced, these quizzes will become more advanced.

As you read the Transcription Quiz letter, decide what punctuation should be used and what words have been omitted from the shorthand.

Then make a shorthand copy of the letter, inserting in your notes the correct punctuation and the missing words.

Do not make any marks in the book itself. If you do, you will destroy the value of these Transcription Quizzes to anyone else who uses the book.

For you to supply: 7 commas — 2 commas conjunction, 3 commas parenthetical, 2 commas series; 2 words missing from the shorthand.

8.

(136)

► **Warmup.** A profitable way to use the few minutes between the time you enter the shorthand classroom and the time your teacher starts the day's lesson is to "warm up." Unless your teacher instructs you otherwise, turn to phrase letter No. 2 on page 13 and see how fast you can copy it.

9. Brief-Form Chart. The following chart contains 42 brief forms and derivatives. Because the words are arranged in family groups, you should be able to read the entire chart in about a minute. Can you do it?

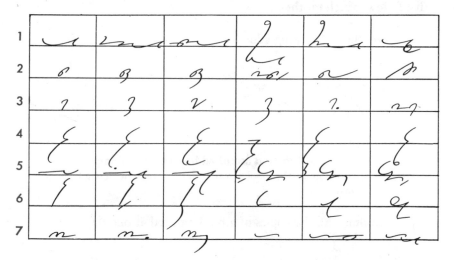

1. Else, someone else, anyone else, everybody else, everyone else, elsewhere.
2. Use, uses, useful, unused, useless, disuse.
3. Wish-usual, wishes, wished, wishful, wishing, unusual.
4. Public-publish, publishing, publisher, unpublished, publications, publicly.
5. Market-Mr., markets-Mrs., marketable, prosecute, prosecution, prosecuted.
6. Subject, subjected, subjective, upon, thereupon, whereupon.
7. Wonder, wondering, wonderful, work, workman, workers.

10. Geographical Expressions

New York, Chicago, Philadelphia, Los Angeles, Boston, Detroit, Cleveland.

Illinois, California, Connecticut, Alabama, Colorado, Arizona, Arkansas.

Reading and Writing Practice

11. Transcription Word Study. The words *addition* and *edition* — because they sound very much alike — occasionally cause difficulty for the stenographer. Those words are used a number of times in the letters that follow; watch for them.

addition Anything added.

The book will make a useful addition to our library.
In addition to the books you ordered, we sent you a desk copy.

edition All the copies of a book printed at one time.

We printed 10,000 copies of the second edition of your book; we have no more copies of the first edition.

12.

whether
edition

addition
library

planning
, parenthetical

, conjunction
investment

(145)

13.

, parenthetical
past due
  no noun,
  no hyphen

customers
overlook
brilliant

offense
, conjunction

different
, conjunction

(120)

14.

, parenthetical
apparently

Philadelphia
, series

enough
nevertheless

, conjunction
accomplish

(119)

15.

fourth
, conjunction

won't
, parenthetical

(70)

Transcription Quiz. For you to supply: 10 commas — 1 comma apposition, 8 commas parenthetical, 1 comma conjunction; 2 missing words.

16.

(134)

23

▶ **Warmup.** A minute or two of warmup will help you get off to a good start on your day's dictation. Turn once again to letter No. 2 on page 13, and copy it as rapidly as you can and still write readable shorthand.

17. Word Families

-come

-long

-count

-mount

Come, income, become, welcome, overcome, outcome.
Long, along, belong, oblong, headlong, prolong.
Count, account, recount, discount, miscount, accountant.
Mount, amount, amounted, dismount, surmount.

Reading and Writing Practice

18. Transcription Word Study. The words *principal* and *principle* are often troublesome to the transcriber. They shouldn't trouble you, however, if you keep in mind the following definitions:

principal (*noun*) Amount of money invested or lent on which interest is paid; the head of a school.

[shorthand]

The principal amounted to $5,000; the interest on that
    principal was $100.
Mr. Smith is principal of North High School.

principal (*adjective*) Main, chief.

[shorthand]

He is the principal stockholder; he owns more than half
    the stock.

principle Rule of action, a law of conduct; a funda-
mental truth.

[shorthand]

I cannot give you any definite principles to guide you.
He is a man of high moral principles.

19. *[shorthand]*

, conjunction
advice

[shorthand]

principal
source

[shorthand]

25

promptly
, conjunction

stockholder
, apposition

, parenthetical
notifying

principles
handling
similar

(158)

20.

whether
persuade

moral
, conjunction

, parenthetical

necessity
, parenthetical

80

, apposition

100

(120)

21.

$87,$

6

10

$7,$

20

$2,$

$4,$

, parenthetical
amounting

$40/$

confident
, parenthetical

(106)

22.

27

, conjunction
appreciated

, parenthetical

30

(94)

Transcription Quiz. For you to supply: 6 commas — 2 commas conjunction, 4 commas parenthetical; 2 missing words.

23.

(123)

► **Warmup.** Don't you find that a minute or two spent on letter No. 2, page 13, before the shorthand period starts really gets you ready for the day's dictation? Turn again to that warmup phrase letter, and write it as rapidly as you can.

24. Word Beginnings and Endings

Re-

De-

Ex-

-ly

-ily, -ally

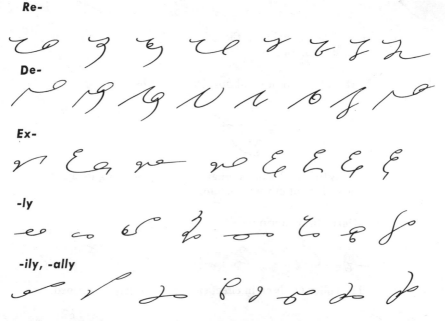

Reply, receive, reserve, replace, receipt, report, repeat, refusal.
Delay, derive, deprive, depend, depart, decide, debate, delight.
Extension, explanation, extreme, extra, express, expect, expression, exception.
Nearly, only, certainly, sufficiently, namely, openly, nicely, badly.
Readily, steadily, family, happily, easily, naturally, finally, vitally.

25. Transcription Word Study. No doubt every English teacher you have had has warned you to be careful of *affect* and *effect*. The following brief definitions will help you determine when to use each word:

affect *(verb)* To act upon, to influence.

[shorthand outline]

Your action will affect both of us vitally.

effect *(noun)* Result, outcome.

[shorthand outline]

Have you thought of the effect of your action on your credit standing?

effect *(verb)* To bring about; to accomplish.

[shorthand outline]

This is the third letter we have written you trying to effect a settlement of your account.

in effect In operation.

[shorthand outline]

The policy has been in effect since the first day we opened.

26. *[shorthand outline]*

adversely
, parenthetical *[shorthand outline]*

, parenthetical
difficulty

, parenthetical
account
reasonable

, parenthetical **(164)**

27.
itself
, conjunction
, parenthetical

, apposition **20**

self-addressed

(76)

28.
effect
received
, parenthetical

, conjunction
extension

past due
  no noun,
  no hyphen

, parenthetical
past-due
  hyphenated
  before noun

affects

(164)

32

29. *[shorthand outlines]*

received

, parenthetical *[shorthand outlines]*

[shorthand outlines] — **30**

, conjunction *[shorthand outlines]*

naturally

[shorthand outlines] 90 *[shorthand]*

[shorthand outlines] **(67)**

Transcription Quiz. For you to supply: 7 commas – 1 comma conjunction, 2 commas series, 4 commas parenthetical; 2 missing words.

30. *[shorthand outlines]*

[shorthand outlines]

[shorthand outlines]

[shorthand outlines]

[shorthand outlines] — 6. *[shorthand outlines]*

[shorthand outlines]

[shorthand outlines]

[shorthand outlines]

[shorthand outlines]

[shorthand outlines] 150/

[shorthand outlines] **(112)**

33

LESSON
5

▶ **Warmup.** Turn once again — for the last time — to letter No. 2 on page 13. The phrases in that letter should now be familiar to you, so familiar in fact that you should be able to write the whole letter in less than 1 minute. Can you do it?

31. Vocabulary Builder

Omission of E in U.

Mt, Md

Ted, Ded

Men, Min, Mon

Amounts

Due, overdue, induce, reduce, produce, new, renew, issue.
Prompt, promptness, empty, blamed, seemed, claimed.
Started, reported, noted, parted, needed, proceeded.
Men, businessmen, many, minute, months.
$4.50; $300; $2,000; 200; 400 **pounds**; 4,000,000; 4,000,000,000;
   $4,000,000,000.

Reading and Writing Practice

32. Transcription Word Study. Most stenographers know the difference between *to*, *two*, and *too*. However, they often use the wrong word through carelessness. To be sure that you use each of these words correctly, read the following definitions and illustrative sentences carefully.

to (*preposition*) In the direction of. (*To* is also used as the sign of the infinitive.)

[shorthand outlines]

We made this lead available to you.
I shall be glad to see you.

two One plus one.

[shorthand outlines]

He took two months for the preparation of his report.

too Also; more than enough.

[shorthand outlines]

Then, too, it is good business to pay your bills promptly.
He had too many problems to be happy.

33. *[shorthand outlines]*

, parenthetical
previously

worried
, conjunction

, conjunction
unreasonable
, parenthetical

34. *(shorthand)* **(124)**

, parenthetical

up to date
no noun,
no hyphen

(shorthand) 1860 *(shorthand)*

(60)

35. *(shorthand)*
believe
overlooked

, conjunction

, parenthetical
   situation
   thanks

(87)

36.

reputation
promptly

first-class
   hyphenated
   before noun

(87)

37.

, parenthetical

(47)

The person who *gets* an attractive stenographic position is the one who has the ability to take dictation rapidly and to transcribe accurately. The person who *holds* that position and uses it for a steppingstone to a more important position, however, is the one who has, in addition, the desirable traits and attitudes that enable him to work smoothly and pleasantly with his fellow workers.

Even though it may be some little time before you are ready for a job in the business world, it is not too early to give serious thought to these traits and attitudes.

In the Reading and Writing Practice of each fifth lesson there is a discussion of these desirable traits and attitudes under the heading "Secretarial Pointer." These discussions will give you an opportunity to find out whether you have these traits and attitudes and, if not, to start developing them. After you read each of these discussions, see whether you can answer the questions in the check lists that follow the shorthand.

38. Pull or Push

(shorthand text)

(235)

Check List

1. How did Ruth do every job that was given to her?
2. What did she do when she had spare time?
3. Sally said she was not paid to do somebody else's work. How do businessmen feel about such an attitude?

Sales

Sales are the lifeblood of a business. A business may manufacture the finest products or may render the best services in the world, but it cannot survive unless it can sell its products or services and make a profit.

The person who is responsible for developing the sales of a company is usually the sales manager. The major part of his job is concerned with two groups of people — the salesmen who work for him and the customers whom the salesmen serve.

In most organizations, the sales manager has complete charge of the salesmen. It is his responsibility to select them, train them, and help them in every way he can to sell his company's products or services. He must see that they are supplied regularly with sales helps and information about the products or services they are selling. Much of the sales manager's correspondence is concerned with the supervision of the sales staff.

Another important phase of the sales manager's job is his contact with the company's customers. Through friendly letters, and often with personal visits, he supplements the efforts of his salesmen and creates and maintains customer good will. He tries to keep the company's present customers happy and, if possible, get them to increase the size of their orders. When a customer stops ordering, the sales manager makes every effort to find out the reason and to regain the customer's business and good will.

The letters and memoranda in this chapter will give you a good sampling of the type of dictation you would take if you were employed in the sales department of an organization.

COMMA BRUSHUP *(Concluded)*

In Chapter 1 you reviewed four of the commas that you studied in the *Gregg Shorthand Manual Simplified.* In Chapter 2 you will review the remaining commas that were presented in that book — commas with introductory expressions. As in the *Gregg Shorthand Manual Simplified,* introductory commas will be treated under the following four headings:

, *when* clause

, *as* clause

, *if* clause

, introductory

All dependent clauses beginning with words other than *when, as,* and *if* will be classified as ", introductory."

> When you go to see him, take along a copy of our catalogue.
>
> As we have done in the past, we shall allow each man $12 a day.
>
> If you find anyone who meets these requirements, please write me.
>
> After he had studied the proposal, he decided to wait.

When the main clause comes first, however, no comma is used between the main clause and the dependent clause.

> Take along a copy of our catalogue when you go to see him.
>
> Please write me if you find anyone who meets these requirements.

A comma is also required after introductory words and explanatory expressions such as *frankly, consequently, on the contrary, for instance.*

> Frankly, we are very much concerned about the loss of your business.
>
> On the contrary, we want to help you in every way we can.

39. Phrase Builder. The following five groups contain 39 phrases. Can you read the entire list in less than a minute?

About

And

Any

As

At

About it, about that, about the, about these, about this, about your, about which, about them, about the matter.

And our, and is, and say, and that, and the, and will, and will be, and will not.

Any information, any more, any one of the, any one of them, any other, any time, any way.

As it is, as the, as they, as it will, as you, as you know, as well, as a result.

At the, at this, at that time, at the time, at all times, at last, at least.

▶ **Warmup Phrase Letter.** The following 116-word letter contains 29 frequently used phrases. Can you read the entire letter in 1 minute?

After you have read it, can you copy it in 2 minutes? This will be your warmup letter while you are working on Chapter 2.

40.

(116)

Reading and Writing Practice

41. Transcription Word Study. Do the words *adopt* and *adapt* give you difficulty? The following explanations and examples should help you to use these words correctly.

adopt To take as one's own; to accept.

I shall adopt the boy from the orphanage.
We were able to adopt many of your suggestions.

adapt To fit, to adjust, to make suitable (usually followed by *to*).

He must be able to adapt himself to being away from home.

Perhaps you may be able to adapt these suggestions to your own selling problems.

42.

, as clause
recommend
requirements

traveling
, conjunction

, if clause
Chicago

(150)

43.

methods
exactly
straight

weather

major

, when clause

, introductory

(147)

45

44.

, apposition
, as clause
joined

recommendation
, introductory

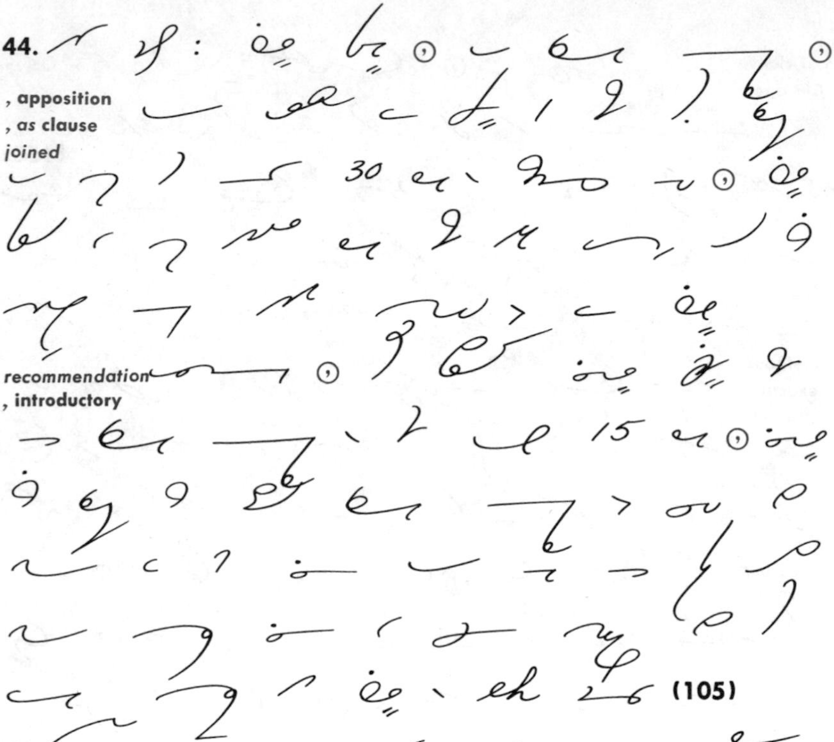

(105)

45.

, introductory

46

, introductory
pleasant

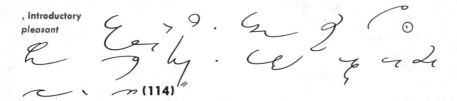

(114)

Transcription Quiz. For you to supply: 6 commas — 1 comma *when* clause, 2 commas series, 2 commas parenthetical, 1 comma conjunction; 2 missing words.

46.

(128)

47

LESSON 7

▶ **Warmup.** For your warmup during the first few minutes of the period, copy letter No. 40 on page 43. Write as rapidly as you can, but be sure that your shorthand notes are readable.

47. Brief-Form Chart. This chart contains 48 brief forms and derivatives. Inasmuch as you have seen all these brief forms many, many times, you should be able to read the entire chart in a minute or less. Can you do it?

1. After, be-by, enclosure, gone, likewise, next.
2. All, been, enough, have, matters, of.
3. Always, between, envelope-nevertheless, he, merchandise, one.
4. Am-more, but, etc., doctors, merchants, opinions.
5. Among, can, every, how-out, mornings, opportunities.
6. A-an, character, for, I, markets-Mrs., otherwise.
7. Are-our-hour, could, from, ideas, must, overcome.
8. At-it, during-Dr., future, in-not, never, property.

48. Geographical Expressions

Des Moines, Seattle, Kansas City, Cincinnati, Buffalo, Duluth, Portland. Florida, Georgia, South Carolina, Indiana, Tennessee, Delaware, Louisiana, Iowa.

Reading and Writing Practice

49. Transcription Word Study. *Personal, personnel.*

personal Individual, private, direct from one person to another.

I wrote him a personal letter.
He is a personal friend of mine.

personnel (*noun*) The people who work for a business or department.

The sales manager is in charge of the sales personnel.

personnel department The department that hires employees.

He applied to the personnel department for a position.

50.

territory
, apposition

Des Moines
, introductory

personnel

ambitious
character
, if clause

good-looking
  hyphenated
  before noun
, when clause

, introductory
initial
career

(154)

51.

death
, apposition

16

, series
friendliness

, series
, when clause

, introductory
experienced

, apposition

, when clause
won't

(157)

52.

assistant
, apposition

51

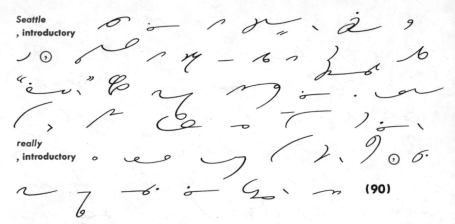

really
, introductory

(90)

Transcription Quiz. For you to supply: 5 commas – 1 comma *if* clause, 2 commas conjunction, 2 commas parenthetical; 2 missing words.

53.

(107)

▶ **Warmup.** Your warmup letter is No. 40 on page 43. Can you copy it faster than you did in the last lesson?

54. Word Families

-prove

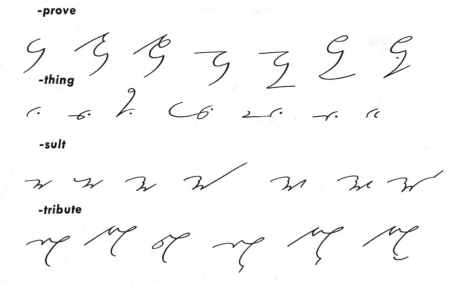

-thing

-sult

-tribute

Prove, disprove, disapprove, improve, improvement, approval, approved.
Thing, anything, everything, plaything, something, nothing, things.
Insult, result, consult, consulted, consultation, consults, consultant.
Contribute, distribute, attribute, contribution, distribution, distributor.

Reading and Writing Practice

55. Transcription Word Study. *Loss, lose, loose.*

loss *(noun)* Something of which one is deprived.

[shorthand]

We regret the loss of your business.

lose *(verb)* To be deprived of.

[shorthand]

We are sorry to lose your business.

loose Unattached, not fastened.

[shorthand]

Why not take him a copy of our loose-leaf catalogue.

56. *[shorthand]*

, conjunction
responsible
loss

[shorthand]

, as clause
business

[shorthand]

, parenthetical
disapproved

[shorthand]

, introductory

[shorthand]

enough
, parenthetical

, parenthetical
afraid

(142)

57.

expressing
some time

realize
, parenthetical

6.

ours
, if clause
disapprove

telephone
grateful

(110)

58.

55

, when clause
probably

, conjunction

, if clause
reason
loss

exception
, conjunction
, if clause

loose-leaf
hyphenated
before noun
, if clause

(134)

59.

, conjunction

, introductory
progress

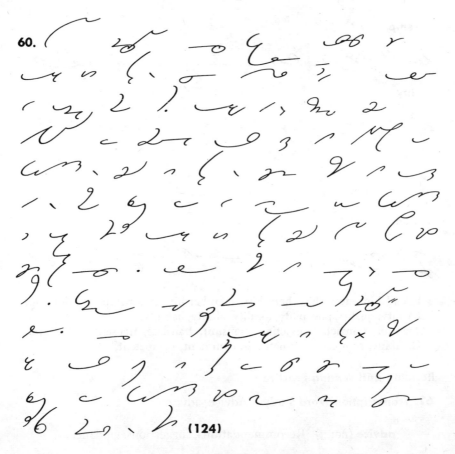

, conjunction
earnestly

(90)

Transcription Quiz. For you to supply: 4 commas—1 comma as clause, 1 comma *if* clause, 2 commas parenthetical; 2 missing words.

60.

(124)

LESSON

9

▶ **Warmup.** Your warmup once again is letter No. 40 on page 43. By this time, you should be familiar with this letter and thus be able to write it rapidly.

61. Word Beginnings and Endings

-ship

-lity

Trans-

Com-

Friendship, steamship, hardship, membership, fellowship, relationship.
Facility, quality, possibility, locality, ability, liability.
Transfer, transact, transaction, transmit, translate, transcribe, transpire.
Combine, complete, competition, comment, competent, complaint.

Reading and Writing Practice

62. Transcription Word Study. *Advice, advise.*

    advice (*noun*) Recommendations, suggestions; guidance.

58

[shorthand symbols]

I appreciate your advice regarding the move we are planning to make.

advise (verb) To guide, to suggest, to inform.

[shorthand symbols]

I should advise you to write him a letter of apology.
Please advise the staff of this proposed move.

63. *[shorthand symbols]*

appreciate
advice

[shorthand symbols]

factors
, introductory
, parenthetical

[shorthand symbols]

effect
, if clause

[shorthand symbols]

, introductory
advise
reactions

(138)

64.

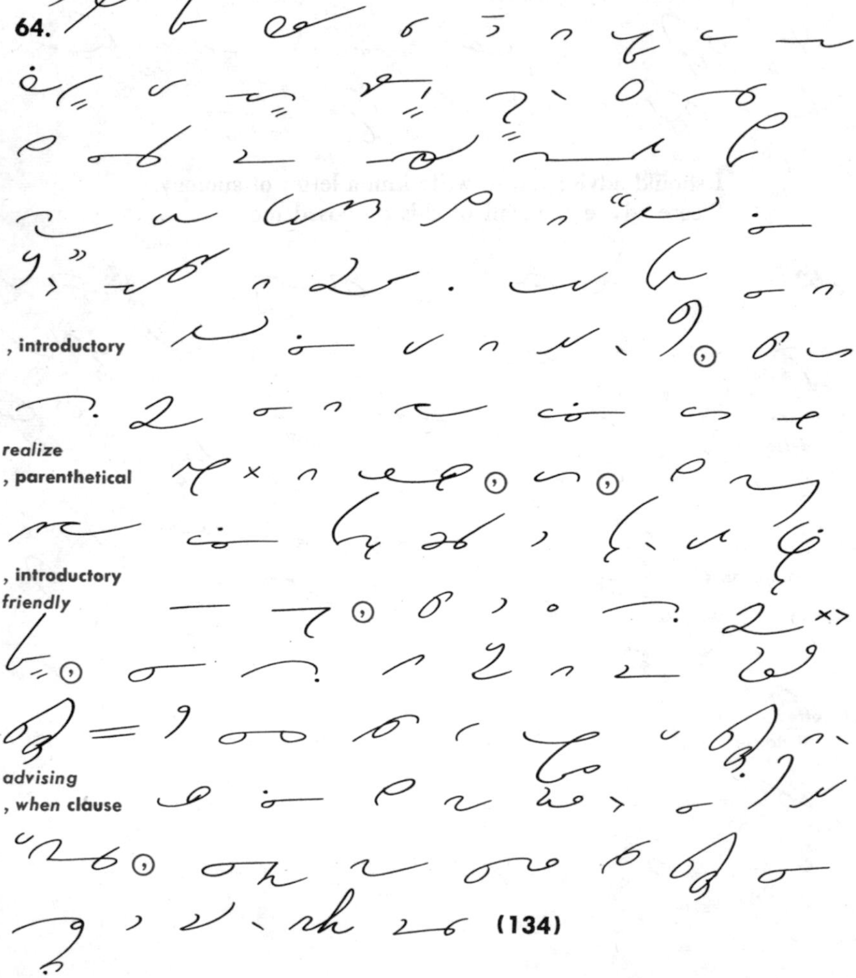

, introductory

realize
, parenthetical

, introductory
friendly

advising
, when clause

(134)

65.

Standard
, as clause

, when clause

(93)

66.

philosopher
, parenthetical

appropriate
, introductory

, if clause
friendship

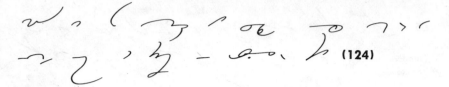

(124)

Transcription Quiz. For you to supply: 7 commas — 3 commas apposition, 2 commas introductory, 1 comma conjunction, 1 comma *if* clause; 2 missing words.

67.

(131)

62

▶ **Warmup.** Copy warmup phrase letter No. 40 on page 43. This will be the last time you will use that letter for your warmup. Do you think you can copy the letter in 1 minute or less?

68. Vocabulary Builder

-tion

Omission of T

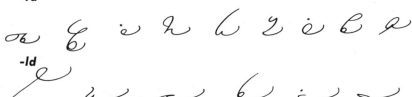

-rd

-ld

Tem

Condition, permission, information, examination, quotation, transportation, commission, session.
Product, respect, fact, expect, protect, select, exact.
Answered, prepared, heard, assured, board, offered, hard, appeared, tired.
Detailed, sold, called, build, hold, yield.
Customer, estimate, temple, temper, temporary, items.

Reading and Writing Practice

69. Transcription Word Study. *Accept, except.*

accept To take.

[shorthand outline]

We shall not accept any orders until January 2.

except (preposition) Omitted; left out.

[shorthand outline]

The report was complete in all details except one.

70. *[shorthand outline]*

competitors
worried

[shorthand outline]

, when clause
anxiety

[shorthand outline]

except
, parenthetical

[shorthand outline]

accepting
, introductory

[shorthand outline]

(147)

71.

inquiry
, apposition

quotation
, series

, conjunction
prompted

well-known
hyphenated
before noun
, parenthetical

estimate
requirements

(127)

Secretarial Pointer

There is a right way and a wrong way to answer the telephone. It pays to learn how to use the telephone to the best advantage, as you will see when you read the case of "Helen on the Telephone."

72. Helen on the Telephone

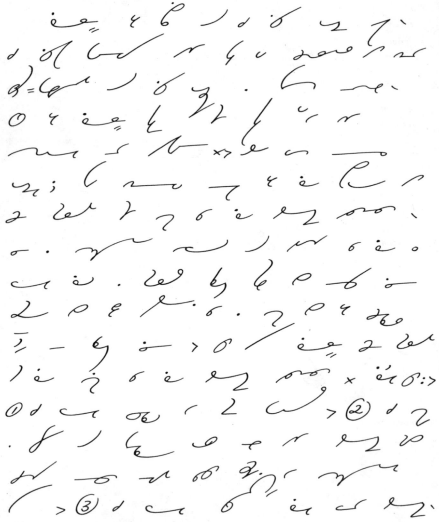

[shorthand notes] × (246)

Check List

1. Why did customers like to talk with Helen on the telephone?
2. Why did Helen keep a pad and pencil next to her telephone?
3. Why was Helen always cheerful and friendly on the telephone even though she herself was feeling neither friendly nor cheerful?

CHAPTER Three

Adjustments

No matter how hard a company may try to keep its customers happy by providing the finest merchandise and the best service, there will be times when misunderstandings will arise between customer and company. Many organizations consider the good will of their customers so important that they have a special department to correct these misunderstandings.

This department usually has a staff of trained "trouble shooters" whose job it is to investigate complaints and to make adjustments that will be fair to both customer and company. Perhaps the most important qualification for a position in this department is the ability to write courteous and convincing letters.

The easiest letters of adjustment to write are those in which the customer's request is granted. The adjustment letter that calls for real skill, however, is the one in which the correspondent must say "No" and make the customer like it.

While letters of complaint result in a great deal of expense and trouble, they also serve a very useful purpose to the business executive. They bring to his attention the things that are wrong in the operation of his business, in the quality of his merchandise, and in the performance and the attitudes of the people who work for him. They show him where he can make improvements that will result in greater customer satisfaction.

In this chapter you will practice on the types of letters and memoranda that will come over your desk if you are a stenographer or secretary in an adjustment department.

✔ NEW MARGINAL REMINDERS

In this chapter you will take up four new pointers of punctuation, typing style, and spelling—the most common use of the semicolon; the typing of dates and amounts; and the apostrophe. These new pointers will be used many times in your practice material so that you will have every opportunity to learn to use them correctly.

; because of comma

As you already know, a comma is used to separate two independent clauses that are joined by one of the conjunctions *and, but, or,* and *nor.* Example:

> Mr. Lee will make an automobile trip through the Southwest, and he should arrive in your city by the end of the month.

Sometimes, however, a comma occurs within one or both of the independent clauses. When that occurs, a semicolon is used between the independent clauses. Examples:

> Our representative, Mr. Lee, will make an automobile trip through the Southwest; and he should arrive in your city by the end of the month.
> Mr. Lee will make an automobile trip through the Southwest; and, weather permitting, he should arrive in your city by the end of the month.

The reason for this is simple enough. If there are other commas in the sentence, something stronger than a comma is required to separate the two parts of the sentence.

The apostrophe

No doubt you know how to use the apostrophe correctly with possessives; but when you write or type, you often forget to insert it. Therefore, to keep you "apostrophe conscious," the apostrophe will appear many times in the lessons that follow. Examples:

Mr. Brown's complaint was disposed of satisfactorily. We hope you will find a few minutes' time to read this.

Dates

The correct form for transcribing dates is October 20, without the th after the figures, when the month precedes the day. The reminder in the margin will read:

Transcribe:
October 20

Amounts

The correct form for transcribing even amounts of dollars is $185 with no decimal point and no ciphers. The reminder in the margin will read:

Transcribe:
$185

73. Phrase Builder. The following five groups contain 41 phrases. Can you read the entire list in about a minute?

By

Do

Each

Few

For

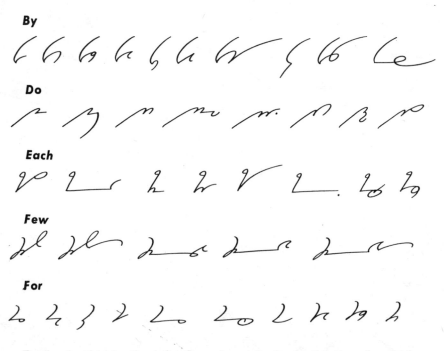

By the, by this, by these, by those, by us, by its, by this time, by which, by that time, by mail.

Do not, do not have, do you, do you know, do you think, do this, do so, do that.

Each day, each month, each one, each other, each time, each morning, each night, each case.

Few days, few days ago, few minutes, few months, few months ago.

For any, for instance, for his, for it, for me, for my, for our, for those, for these, for you.

▶ **Warmup Phrase Letter.** The following 148-word letter contains 30 frequently used phrases.

This will be your warmup letter while you are working on Chapter 3.

74.

(148)

Reading and Writing Practice

75. Transcription Word Study. Sometimes the simplest words give us the most difficulty — not because we do not understand them, but because we are likely to be a little careless in their use. *Hear* and *here* are examples.

hear To gain knowledge, to be informed.

[shorthand]

We were sorry to hear that you wish to return the dress.

here In this place.

[shorthand]

Here is the dress that you ordered.

here and there In one place or another.

[shorthand]

We have been able to pick up some interesting information here and there.

76.
Transcribe:
November 15
, introductory

[shorthand]

; because of comma
, parenthetical
unfortunately

[shorthand]

, introductory
consequently

[shorthand]

, introductory
; because of comma

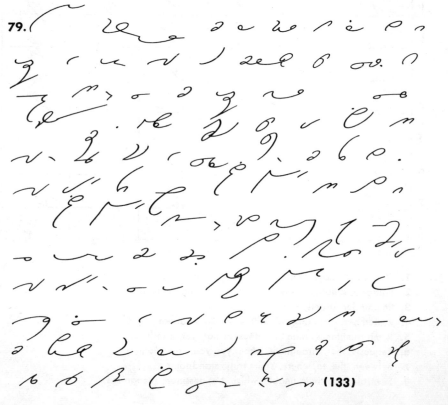

, parenthetical

Transcribe:
$12

(65)

Transcription Quiz. For you to supply: 6 commas — 2 commas conjunction, 2 commas when clause, 1 comma parenthetical, 1 comma introductory; 2 missing words.

79.

(133)

LESSON
12

▶ **Warmup.** For your warmup during the first few minutes of the period, copy letter No. 74 on page 72. Write as rapidly as you can, but be sure that your shorthand notes are readable.

80. Brief-Form Chart. The following chart contains 48 brief forms and derivatives. Can you read the entire chart in a minute or less?

1						
2						
3						
4						
5						
6						
7						
8						

1. Quantities, should, every, very, why, individuals.
2. Railroad, situations, any, wanted, wondering, merchants.
3. Remainder, streets, they, was, would, once.
4. Remember, such, this, will-well, yesterday, cannot.
5. Remit-remittance, than-then, those, what, yet, goodness.
6. Requests, that, throughout, when, you-your, questioning.
7. Between, the, to, where, Yours truly, standpoint.
8. Several, there-their, unable, which, businessman, recognizes.

81. Geographical Expressions

St. Louis, Washington, Newark, New Orleans, Denver, Akron, Syracuse. New Jersey, Minnesota, Kansas, Oregon, Pennsylvania, Ohio, Maryland, Wyoming.

Reading and Writing Practice

82. Transcription Word Study. *Later, latter.*

later By and by; in the future.

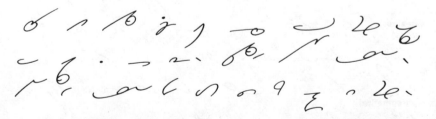

You will be hearing from us later in the week.
We shall be glad to send you the information later.

latter Of two things, being the one mentioned second; belonging to the end of a period of time.

I had to decide whether to have my old furnace repaired or to buy a new one. I decided to do the latter.
During the latter part of this week, I shall inspect your furnace.

83.

naturally
, introductory

, conjunction

, introductory
appreciate

, if clause
envelope

84.

(118)

, as clause
Newark

latter
, parenthetical

; because of comma
, parenthetical
estimate

(115)

85.
, as clause
, apposition
residence

necessary
, parenthetical
; because of comma

165/

, introductory
, parenthetical

(125)

86.

Transcribe:
April 16
whether

, conjunction

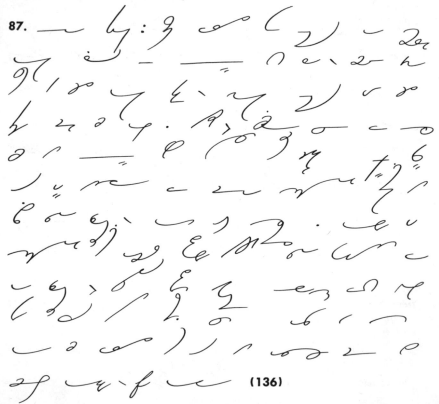

6.

, introductory
; because of comma
, parenthetical

(110)

Transcription Quiz. For you to supply: 9 commas—1 comma as clause, 4 commas parenthetical, 1 comma introductory, 2 commas series, 1 comma conjunction; 2 missing words.

87.

(136)

▶ **Warmup.** Can you copy warmup letter No. 74 on page 72 faster than you did yesterday? Each day, try to cut a few seconds off your copying time.

88. Word Families

-ken

-duction

-rate

-ary

Taken, weaken, spoken, broken, darken, awaken, quicken.
Reduction, production, introduction, induction, reproduction, deduction.
Overrate, operate, separate, desperate, decorate, accurate, crate.
Salary, sanitary, secretary, primary, summary, customary.

Reading and Writing Practice

89. Transcription Word Study. *Weather, whether.*

weather State of the air or atmosphere with respect to heat or cold, wetness or dryness; climate.

If we have good weather, we will deliver your table on
Wednesday.
My cold was aggravated by the bad weather.

whether Indicating a choice (often followed by or);
also used to introduce an indirect question.

We will inspect the desk to see whether or not the drawers
can be adjusted.
Let me know whether we should send it to your office or
to your home.

90.
owe
grippe
, conjunction

, when clause
, apposition
spare

; because of comma
, parenthetical
completely

overrate
, conjunction

, conjunction
further

(137)

91.

Transcribe:
March 6
son's

acknowledging
crated
, as clause

weather
, introductory
, apposition

20.

first-class
hyphenated
before noun

(121)

92.

referred
distressed
, if clause

repairs
, if clause

, if clause

(104)

93.

Transcribe:
 December 15

, conjunction
weather

, as clause
ours

corrected
, when clause

(118)

Transcription Quiz. For you to supply: 8 commas — 1 comma conjunction, 1 comma *when* clause, 1 comma *as* clause, 2 commas parenthetical, 2 commas apposition, 1 comma introductory; 2 missing words.

94.

(137)

LESSON

14

▶ **Warmup.** Can you copy letter No. 74 on page 72 a little faster than you did yesterday? If there is time to do so, copy the letter a second time in your best shorthand, for control.

95. Word Beginnings and Endings

-ble

-cal

Un-

Fur-

Sensible, available, terrible, payable, capable, desirable, impossible, suitable.
Physical, medical, critical, practical, mechanical, technical.
Unfair, unfilled, unjust, unpaid, unreasonable, unsatisfactory, until.
Furniture, furnish, furnished, furnishings, unfurnished, furnace, furnaces, furlough.

Reading and Writing Practice

96. Transcription Word Study. *It's, its.*

it's The contraction of *it is.*

[shorthand outline]

It's his intention to serve you in every way that he can.

its (no apostrophe!) Possessive form meaning belonging to it.

[shorthand outline]

In its present form, the report is not satisfactory.

97. *[shorthand]*

except
its

[shorthand]

, introductory
; because of comma
furniture

[shorthand]

, parenthetical
truckman

[shorthand]

(91)

98. *[shorthand]*

passed
bedroom

[shorthand]

, when clause
adjust

, parenthetical
inconvenienced
deed

Transcribe:
$40
; because of comma

; because of comma

, series
, conjunction

(135)

99.
, introductory
; because of comma
intention

, conjunction
accept

(62)

100.
, as clause
St. Louis

dye
, introductory

contact
moist

(83)

101.

, apposition

, when clause
plain

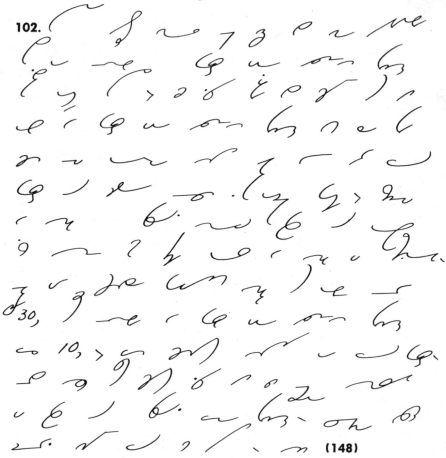

(133)

Transcription Quiz. For you to supply: 8 commas – 1 comma conjunction, 1 comma as clause, 2 commas series, 2 commas introductory, 2 commas parenthetical; 2 missing words.

102.

(148)

► **Warmup.** This will be the last time that you will copy letter No. 74 on page 72 as a warmup. If you have time, copy the letter a second time in your best shorthand, for control.

103. Vocabulary Builder

-ther

W in the Body of a Word

Nt, Nd

Ow

Ort

Neither, further, whether, leather, father, gather, grandfather.
Quick, dwell, equipped, Broadway, quote, square, queen.
Print, recent, entire, entry, sent, center, explained, bind.
Now, cow, south, voucher, crowd, proud, doubtless.
Port, export, report, import, transport, quart, quarter, sort.

Reading and Writing Practice

104. Transcription Word Study.   Proceed, precede.

proceed   To go forward or onward; to advance.

> We cannot proceed with the work until we have further
> information.

precede   To go before in rank or importance or in order
of time.

He will precede me as a speaker on the program.

105.

, introductory
bindery

different
, conjunction

, conjunction
distribution

uneasy
proceed

(152)

106.

, apposition
Transcribe:
November 3

236

12

last-minute
hyphenated
before noun

urgently
, conjunction

(146)

Secretarial Pointer

An office worker will not always have ideal conditions under which to work. The person who gets ahead, however, is the one who adjusts himself cheerfully to the conditions that he finds and does the best he can under the circumstances. Mary, in the following article, was a cheerful "adjuster" and was well rewarded as a result.

107. Mary Adjusts to the Job

(240)

Check List

1. Why did Mary have to use five or six different typewriters every day?

2. How did Mary respond when her employers told her they could not immediately give her a desk and a typewriter of her own?

3. Why did Mary receive several promotions in two years?

CHAPTER FOUR

Personnel

If you should apply for a position with a fairly large company when you are graduated from school, it is quite likely that your first contact with that company will be through the personnel department. This department is usually under the direction of a personnel manager. In very large companies, he may have several assistants, all of whom are especially trained in handling people.

The personnel department of a company has two major jobs: (1) To see that the company is supplied with well-trained workers, so that it can operate efficiently. (2) To look after the interests and comfort of those workers, so that they are happy in their work — as happy workers are productive workers.

After a worker has been hired, a member of the personnel department usually tries to make him feel at home. He tells him about the business — the products it makes, the services it renders, the people who run it, and the part the new worker will play in the operation of the business. Often he will take the new worker through the building and introduce him to the people with whom he will come in contact.

In addition, the member of the personnel department explains the various benefits that the worker will enjoy — paid vacations, insurance, social activities, etc. — as well as the company rules and regulations, which he will be expected to observe.

The letters and memoranda that you will practice in this chapter are representative types of material that pass through the hands of the stenographer who works in the personnel department of an organization.

NEW MARGINAL REMINDERS (Concluded)

In this chapter you will take up three new marginal reminders: (1) another use of the semicolon, (2) the typing of street addresses, (3) the use of a period at the end of a sentence that makes a courteous request in the form of a question. These are the last of the new marginal reminders with which you will deal in *Gregg Dictation Simplified*.

In the remaining chapters, these new marginal reminders, as well as all those that you have previously studied, will be used again and again so that you will have the best possible opportunity to learn their correct application.

; no conjunction

A semicolon is used to separate two independent, but closely related, clauses when no conjunction is used to connect the clauses.

> Mary received an appointment in the personnel department; her sister was not appointed.

The above sentence could be written as two sentences.

> Mary received an appointment in the personnel department. Her sister was not appointed.

Because the two thoughts are closely related, however, the use of the semicolon seems more appropriate.

Street address

The form of street address recommended for use in your transcripts is "138 East 36 Street"—without *th* after *36*, you will notice.

The practice of omitting *th*, *st*, and *d* from numbered street names is growing, because the omission of these endings adds to the readability of the address.

The marginal reminder for the foregoing address would be:

> Transcribe:
> *36 Street*

Very often one businessman may wish to persuade another to take some definite action. He could make his request for action with a direct statement, such as:

> I want to hear from you by return mail.

A direct statement of this type, however, might antagonize the reader. Many businessmen, therefore, prefer to make such a request in the form of a question.

> May I hear from you by return mail.

Where a request for definite action is put in the form of a question, a period is used at the end of the sentence.

This is how you can decide whether to use a question mark or a period:

1. If the question calls for an answer in the form of *action*, use a period.

2. If the question calls for an answer in the form of *words*, use a question mark.

108. Phrase Builder. The following four groups of phrases contain 48 frequently used business phrases. Can you read the entire list in a minute and a half or less?

From

Has

He

I

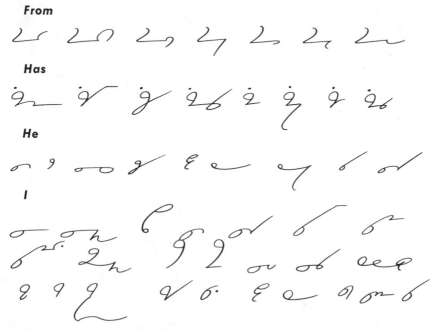

From the, from this, from us, from which, from you, from his, from our.

Has come, has done, has had, has made, has not, has not been, has the, has not yet.

He can, he is, he may, he said, he was, he will, he will be, he would, he could.

I am, I am sure, I believe, I can, I could, I did not, I do not, I do not think, I feel sure, I have, I have not, I know, I need, I realize, I saw, I shall, I shall be glad, I should, I think, I was, I will, I wish, I wonder, I would.

► **Warmup Phrase Letter.** The following 130-word warmup phrase letter contains 30 phrases. Your reading goal: 1½ minutes; your writing goal: 2 minutes.

109.

(130)

Reading and Writing Practice

110. Transcription Word Study. *Choose, chose.*

   choose   To select.

[shorthand outline]

Any day that you choose will be satisfactory to me.

chose (past tense of *choose*)   Selected.

[shorthand outline]

I chose commercial art as my major in high school.

111. *[shorthand]*

, when clause
serious

; no conjunction
stenographers

commercial
label
, series

, introductory
; because of comma

, if clause
samples

(160)

112.

graduation
traveling
, introductory

22

education
settled

won't
. courteous
request

(117)

113. 15

Transcribe:
January 15

(68)

Transcription Quiz. For you to supply: 9 commas — 2 commas conjunction, 4 commas parenthetical, 1 comma *if* clause, 2 commas series; 2 missing words.

114.

(157)

LESSON 17

▶ **Warmup.** Your warmup letter is No. 109 on page 100. This time, instead of warming up on the entire letter, use only the first paragraph. Write slowly at first, in your best penmanship. Write the paragraph again, writing as rapidly as you can. If time permits, write it a third time, striving for an even higher writing speed. Finally, write the paragraph slowly for control.

115. Brief-Form Chart. The following brief-form chart contains 42 brief forms and derivatives. Reading goal: 1 minute or less.

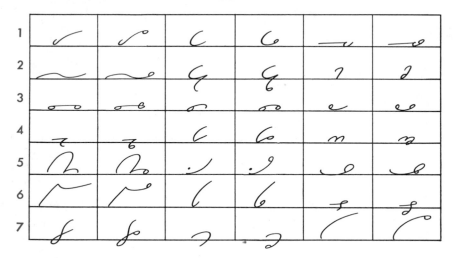

1. Ordinary, ordinarily, present, presently, most, mostly.
2. Glad, gladly, purpose, purposely, usual-wish, usually.
3. Immediate, immediately, week-weak, weekly-weakly, year, yearly.
4. Instant-instance, instantly, part, partly-party, world, worldly.
5. Difficult, difficulty, hand, handy, like, likely.
6. Deliver, delivery, body, bodily, necessary, necessarily.
7. Particular, particularly, confident-confidence, confidently, time, timely.

116. Geographical Expressions

[shorthand outlines]

Milwaukee, Jersey City, Knoxville, San Antonio, Omaha, Richmond, Baltimore.

Wisconsin, Nevada, New Mexico, Mississippi, Virginia, West Virginia, Wyoming, Idaho.

Reading and Writing Practice

117. Transcription Word Study. Correspondence, correspondents.

correspondence Letters and memoranda.

[shorthand outlines]

The file clerk could not find the correspondence in the files.

correspondents Persons who write letters.

[shorthand outlines]

I was one of the correspondents in a large mail-order house.

118. *[shorthand outlines]*

submitting
correspondents
offered

[shorthand outlines]

successor
; no conjunction

, parenthetical
, apposition
January

(146)

119.

, introductory
supervisor
Milwaukee

, introductory

; because of comma
, series
memorandum

, when clause
Transcribe:
$300

Spelling and Punctuation Check List

In your shorthand class you are improving your ability to spell and punctuate as well as building up your shorthand skill. Are you careful, however, to spell and punctuate correctly when you

1. Write compositions, reports, and assignments in your other subjects?

2. Correspond with friends to whom you must write in longhand or on the typewriter?

Make correct spelling and punctuation a habit!

worth-while
  hyphenated
  before noun
, introductory

(160)

120.
, apposition
three-month
  hyphenated
  before noun

Hart's
nursing
, conjunction

employee
; no conjunction

, parenthetical
recommendation

(100)

Transcription Quiz. For you to supply: 10 commas — 3 commas apposition, 2 commas *if* clause, 1 comma *as* clause, 4 commas parenthetical; 2 missing words.

121.

(153)

▶ **Warmup.** Your warmup letter is again No. 109, page 100. Did you like the new warmup procedure in Lesson 17? Why not warm up on paragraph 2 of the letter in the same way that you warmed up on paragraph 1 in Lesson 17.

122. Word Families

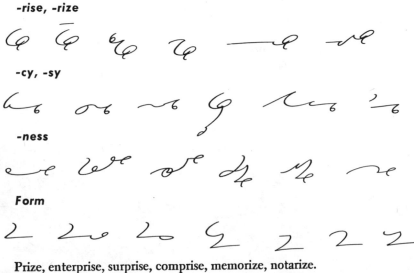

-rise, -rize

-cy, -sy

-ness

Form

Prize, enterprise, surprise, comprise, memorize, notarize.
Policy, accuracy, courtesy, privacy, diplomacy, supremacy.
Illness, friendliness, kindness, faithfulness, thoughtfulness, goodness.
Form, formerly, formally, perform, inform, conform, reform.

Reading and Writing Practice

123. Transcription Word Study. *Formerly, formally.*

formerly   Before, in the past.

(shorthand outline)

Formerly, the office was open until noon; now it is open all day.

formally   In the regular way, according to established custom or form.

We have been formally notified that the services of the Medical Department will be expanded.

124.   _(shorthand outline)_

, parenthetical
summarize
functions

, introductory

full-time
  hyphenated
  before noun
, introductory

, introductory
physical

authorized

(3)

, if clause
policies

(154)

125.

welcome
formally

pleasant
, conjunction

, series
, parenthetical
natural

; because of comma
beginner

, parenthetical
succeed

126.

inquiries
discounts

familiar
, introductory

40,

, introductory
, series
technical

, introductory

20,

25,

10,

127.

Directors
liberal

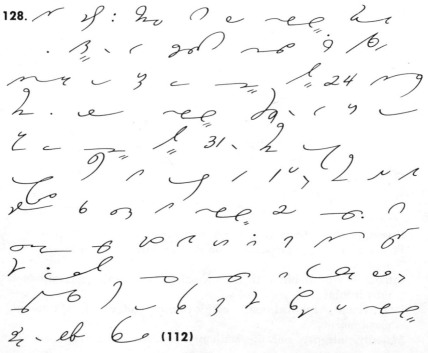

(107)

Transcription Quiz. For you to supply: 8 commas—1 comma as clause, 3 commas apposition, 2 commas parenthetical, 2 commas introductory; 2 missing words.

128.

(112)

LESSON
19

▶ **Warmup.** Your warmup letter is No. 109 on page 100. Practice the last two paragraphs as you practiced paragraph 1 in Lesson 17 and paragraph 2 in Lesson 18. Don't forget the final writing for control.

129. Word Beginnings and Endings

Per-

Pro-

Inter-, Intr-

-ment

-rity

Person, personal, personnel, permit, permission, performance, perfect.

Promote, provide, proposal, promise, approach, reproach, approve, approval.

Interest, interested, international, internal, interview, interrupt, introduce, introduction.

Department, appointment, employment, judgment, statement, management.

Majority, integrity, sincerity, authority, security, minority, superiority.

Reading and Writing Practice

130. Transcription Word Study. *Quite, quiet.*

Here is another pair of words that stenographers often mistranscribe, usually because of carelessness. In *quiet*, the e comes *before* the *t*; in *quite*, the e comes *after* the *t*. (Also be careful of *quit*, in which there is no e.)

quite   Completely, entirely.

His character is quite above reproach.
You are quite correct in your statement.

quiet   Not excited, calm, free from noise.

He is a quiet young man, who is not easily hurried.
We shall have dinner in our quiet dining room.

131.

; because of comma
, series
qualifications

115

reproach
, conjunction

. courteous
   request
; no conjunction

, as clause **(131)**

132.

Transcribe:
   17 Street

, parenthetical
friendly

, parenthetical
approval

, as clause
mind

quiet **(117)**

133.

Transcribe:
January 3

, conjunction
temporary
eager

Green's
, parenthetical

nevertheless
, introductory

sincerity
, introductory
; because of comma

(145)

134.

advice
secretary

117

, conjunction

well-trained
   hyphenated
   before noun

beginning
Transcribe:
   $300

(88)

Transcription Quiz.   For you to supply: 7 commas — 3 commas introductory, 2 commas parenthetical, 1 comma as clause, 1 comma conjunction; 2 missing words.

135.

6-4516

(142)

▶ **Warmup.** Your warmup letter for the last time is No. 109, page 100. Copy the entire letter as many times as you can and as rapidly as you can.

136. Vocabulary Builder

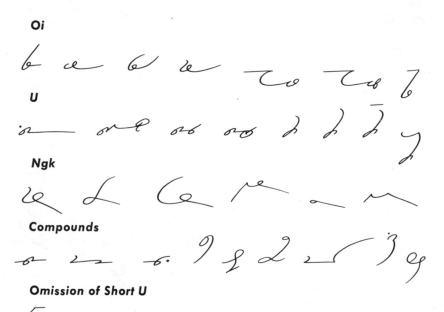

Oi

U

Ngk

Compounds

Omission of Short U

Join, oil, point, soil, employ, employee, enjoy.
Human, utilize, unit, unite, few, view, interview, review.
Frank, bank, blank, drink, ink, trunk.
Anyone, someone, anything, however, thereafter, everywhere, sometime, whoever, wherever.
Done, lunch, come, son, some, run, welcome.

137. Transcription Word Study. *Assistance, assistants.*

assistance Help.

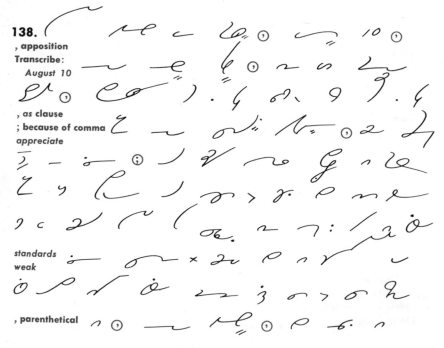

He will be glad to give you any assistance you need.

assistants Helpers.

The personnel director and his assistants talked to the new group of workers.

138.

, apposition
Transcribe:
August 10

, as clause
; because of comma
appreciate

standards
weak

, parenthetical

grateful
; because of comma
, if clause

(143)

139.

, if clause
Union

; no conjunction
, introductory

, introductory
full-time
part-time
  hyphenated
  before noun

, if clause
, apposition
weekday

9   5

Transcribe: / 416   67
  67 Street
  (145)

Informal dress may be entirely satisfactory for school, but it won't do for a business office. Businessmen expect their workers to be properly and neatly dressed when they are in the office; therefore, it will pay you to find out what the well-dressed business girl wears. In the following secretarial hint, Grace Smith was not properly dressed – and see what happened!

140. Business Dress

(Shorthand outline) **(262)**

Check List

1. What did Grace wear in the office that was objectionable to her employer?

2. What excuse did Grace give for wearing sweaters and skirts?

3. Why did Grace decide to change her manner of dressing for the office?

THE CHAMPION'S NOTES

When Martin J. Dupraw won the world's shorthand championship, he established some remarkable records for accuracy. On a speech dictated at 200 words a minute for five minutes, he made only one error. On court testimony dictated at 280 words a minute for five minutes, he made only two errors. These and many other records that he has established are due, in large measure, to the amazing legibility of his shorthand notes.

When you examine Mr. Dupraw's shorthand notes on the following page, which he wrote from dictation especially for *Gregg Dictation Simplified*, one thing will immediately impress you — the careful attention to proportion.

Notice for example how large he makes his *a* circles and how small he makes the *e* circles. There is never any question whether a circle represents *a* or *e*. Notice, too, how much larger his *l*'s are than his *r*'s. As you read Mr. Dupraw's notes, you will observe many other examples of good proportion.

Another thing that will strike you as you examine Mr. Dupraw's notes is the way he rounds off angles. He does not consciously do this; rounding angles comes naturally to him as a result of his high speed. As your speed increases, you, too, will find that you will naturally round off angles.

In the piece that Mr. Dupraw has written in his beautiful shorthand, he discusses the size of notes. You will notice that he has a fairly large shorthand style, just as he has a large longhand style.

Don't try to imitate Mr. Dupraw's style of writing; take the advice he gives in his article "How Big Should My Shorthand Be?"

PART TWO

Taking New-Matter Dictation

BY THIS TIME, you are no doubt taking dictation on new material, material that you have not previously practiced. If you have been doing the lessons in this book faithfully — and will continue to do so — your ability to write new matter will develop rapidly, and you will experience a real thrill as you find yourself taking dictation at faster and faster rates of speed.

Here are some suggestions that will be helpful to you in taking new-matter dictation:

During dictation, don't stop to improve an outline once you have written it. Every shorthand writer, no matter how skillful he may be, will occasionally write a poor outline during dictation. When you do this, do not make the mistake of scratching out the outline and rewriting it. The dictator will not wait while you are "patching up" your notes, and you may find yourself hopelessly behind as a result. Once you have written an outline, leave it. Even though you may have written it poorly, in most cases when you transcribe you will be able to decipher it with the aid of the context.

When the dictator uses a word that is unfamiliar to you, write something down — don't stop writing. In your practice work and in your dictation on the job, you will constantly be encountering words that are unfamiliar to you. When one of these words comes along, try to write it in full; write all the sounds you hear. If you cannot do this, try to get down at least the beginning. Often this beginning, along with the context, will be sufficient to enable you to find the correct word in the dictionary.

There will be times when you are unable to write anything for an unfamiliar word. When that happens, leave a space in your notes and continue writing. Don't spend so much time trying to form an outline for the word that the dictation gets too far ahead of you. You will be surprised, when you transcribe, how often you will be able to fill in the word or supply an equally acceptable one — with the aid of the context.

Never stop writing. There will be times in your speed-development work when the dictation will be too fast for you and you will miss some of it. You must not let this worry you. If you always took dictation at speeds that you could write easily, you would make little progress. In order to build up your speed, you must practice at speeds beyond the rate that you are writing at the moment. When you find yourself getting behind the dictator, hang on as long as you can. Something may happen that will enable you to catch up — the dictator may stop to take a breath or there may be an easy spot in the dictation or a nice phrase may come to your rescue.

If, however, you are so far behind that you feel nothing will help you, drop the words that you have not yet written and pick up the dictation again. But don't decide to drop too soon — and never stop writing!

Don't try to phrase too much. Some writers have the feeling that the key to shorthand speed is phrasing. Phrases will help in gaining shorthand speed only if they can be written without hesitation.

Remember, too, that a dictator may not always say a phrase as one piece. He may say one word in a phrase and then pause before he says the remaining words. When that occurs, you will probably have the first word written before you hear the rest of the phrase. You should then write the remaining words of the phrase as though no phrase were involved. Under no circumstances should you scratch out the word that you have already written and then write the phrase.

Automobiles

When Henry Ford placed his "horseless carriage" on the market in 1892, many people scoffed at him. "Just a fad that won't last long," they said, as they continued to ride in their horse-drawn buggies.

But how wrong they were! That "fad" has developed into one of the world's greatest industries and has played a tremendous part in the development and growth of our country. Today, millions of people own cars. For many of them, these cars are not luxuries but necessities.

The automobile is responsible for the employment of millions of people, not only in the automobile industry but also in that vast number of industries that supply the hundreds of items that go into the making of a modern automobile.

Most people, when they think of the workers who have had a hand in getting a car from the production line onto the open road, usually think of engineers, designers, draftsmen, and factory workers. Seldom do they think of the part played by the army of office workers who are responsible for the mountains of paper work that must be done to get a car from the drafting board into the hands of a proud owner. Part of this vast army is made up of thousands upon thousands of secretaries and stenographers, without whose contribution the manufacture and purchase of an automobile would be a difficult, if not an impossible, job.

When you accept your first stenographic position, you will very likely find that the product or service that your employer sells is dependent in one way or another on the automobile.

The letters in this chapter deal with various phases of the automobile industry. You will enjoy building your shorthand speed on these letters.

141. Phrase Builder. The following list contains 35 useful business phrases that you should be able to read in half a minute or less. Many of these phrases are given in your warmup phrase letter and the other letters in this lesson.

Several

So

Thank

That

There

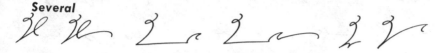

Several days, several days ago, several months, several months ago, several other, several times.

So far, so little, so much, so long, so that, so well.

Thank you, thank you for, thank you for the, thank you for your, thank you for your letter, thank you for your order, thank you for this.

That are, that have, that is, that is not, that it is, that it was, that it will, that it will be, that the.

There are, there is, there was, there will be, there will not be, there has been, there may be.

▶ **Warmup Phrase Letter.** Your warmup letter for this chapter contains 177 words. There are 40 common and useful phrases in it. How fast can you read and copy the letter?

142. *[shorthand outlines]*

(177)

143. Transcription Word Study. In Chapters 1 through 4 you studied pairs of words that might cause you difficulty in transcription. From this point on, your Transcription Word Study will give you brief definitions of words, selected from the Reading and Writing Practice, that may be unfamiliar to you. Be sure to read these definitions before you begin your work on the Reading and Writing Practice.

> **sedan** Two- or four-door car that seats five to seven persons.
>
> **accelerator** The gas pedal.

144.

inquiry

, apposition

accelerator
gently
, series

guide
, if clause

. courteous
request

(116)

145.

, if clause
successful

; no conjunction
sedan

, introductory

, conjunction
year's
model

, parenthetical
quiet

(131)

Transcription Quiz. The transcription quizzes hereafter will be a greater challenge to you in two ways:

1. Thus far you had to supply only commas to punctuate a letter correctly; hereafter, you will also have to supply semicolons. If you have paid close attention to the semicolons in the marginal reminders in Chapters 3 and 4, this new feature will present no problem for you.

2. Thus far you have had to supply missing words that were obvious, as only one possible word made sense in the sentence; hereafter, any one of a number of words will make sense. It will be up to you to supply the word that you think fits best in the sentence. To illustrate:

In the spot where there has been an omission, any one of the following words would be considered correct: *want, wish, like, care.* Assuming that you decide that the word *want* makes the sentence read most smoothly, you would write it in your shorthand notebook thus:

Whatever word you choose, be sure that it makes sense in the sentence.

For you to supply: 6 commas — 2 commas apposition, 1 comma as clause, 2 commas parenthetical, 1 comma conjunction; 1 semicolon because of comma; 2 missing words.

146.

(139)

LESSON 22

▶ **Warmup.** Your warmup letter is No. 142 on page 130. Once again, practice it a paragraph at a time. Today, write the first paragraph slowly the first time; as rapidly as you can the second time; and in your best shorthand the third time.

147. Brief-Form Chart. The following chart contains 48 brief forms and derivatives. Reading goal: 1 minute or less.

1. Returnable, workable, recognizable, desirable, valuable, considerable.
2. Keeper, purchaser, governor, successor, organizer, writer.
3. Particularly, mostly, rightly, probably, immediately, likely.
4. Longer, sooner, bigger, weaker, timer, biller.
5. Considers, desires, instances, corresponds, houses, offices.
6. Advantages, agents, covers, subjects, governs, objects.
7. Reconsider, recover, renumber, redirect, rewrite, rework.
8. Represent, reorganize, re-use, reorder, restate, republic.

148. Geographical Expressions

[shorthand symbols]

Providence, Salt Lake City, Louisville, Columbus, Cleveland.
Iowa, Kentucky, Montana, Nebraska, Rhode Island, South Dakota, Utah,
Vermont.

Reading and Writing Practice

149. Transcription Word Study

appraise Set a value on.

trade-in allowance The amount a dealer will allow on
an old car toward the purchase of a new car.

ignition system The electrical system of a car that con-
trols starting, lights, etc.

150. *[shorthand outlines]*

, as clause
, apposition
appraise

[shorthand outlines]

, parenthetical
ignition

first-class
hyphenated
before noun
, introductory

[shorthand outlines]

, introductory

trade-in
  hyphenated
  before noun

(140)

151.

privilege
license

lapse
, introductory

, when clause
answer
, series

envelope
, introductory

season's
Christmas

(118)

152.

, as clause
pleasant

, conjunction
renewal

won't
. courteous
request

; no conjunction
requires

(113)

153.

assistance
ditch
Route

15/

wrecking
its

41

505

carried
convey

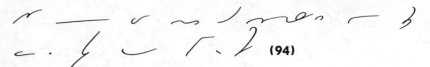

(94)

Transcription Quiz. For you to supply: 4 commas — 2 commas introductory, 2 commas parenthetical; 2 semicolons — 1 semicolon because of comma, 1 semicolon no conjunction; 2 missing words.

154.

(149)

▶ **Warmup.** Use paragraph 2 of letter No.142, page 130, today for your warmup. Remember, write the paragraph slowly on your first writing; then as rapidly as you can without making your shorthand unreadable; and finally in your best shorthand, for control.

155. Word Families

-ple

-most

-ious

-quent

Ample, sample, example, people, triple, principle.
Most, foremost, utmost, uppermost, almost, mostly.
Serious, various, curious, victorious, previous, obvious, tedious, studious.
Frequent, frequently, infrequent, infrequently, subsequent, subsequently, eloquent.

Reading and Writing Practice

156. Transcription Word Study

tread The grooved surface of the tire; the part of a tire that actually touches the road.

snow tire A tire with a special tread that enables a car to ride with safety over snow-covered roads.

cord The fabric used in the making of a tire.

157. [shorthand outlines]

, apposition
salesmen's

, introductory
; no conjunction
, introductory

, parenthetical
well known
  no noun,
  no hyphen

, introductory

, as clause
; because of comma
recommend

(141)

158. [shorthand outlines]

50,

, introductory
, apposition
difference

wheels
, parenthetical
, when clause

pair
. courteous
   request

(105)

159.

appointments
weather
reason

cope
, series

, **introductory**
developed

. courteous
request   **(144)**

160.

low-priced
hyphenated
before noun

, **introductory**
usage
rough

, **introductory**
safety
equipped

142

(118)

Transcription Quiz. For you to supply: 5 commas — 2 commas *if* clause, 2 commas series, 1 comma *when* clause; 1 semicolon no conjunction; 2 missing words.

161.

(146)

LESSON 24

▶ **Warmup.** For today's warmup, use paragraph 3 of letter No. 142 on page 130. Copy the paragraph slowly, then rapidly, and finally in your best shorthand.

162. Word Beginnings and Endings

Con-

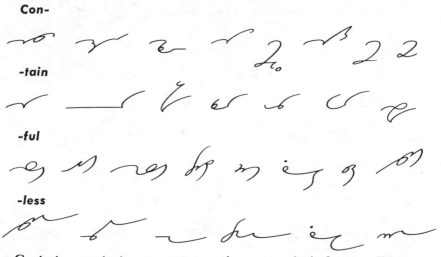

-tain

-ful

-less

Contact, constant, concern, continue, convincingly, conditions, convenient, confer.

Contain, maintain, obtain, certain, retain, pertain, captain.

Careful, thoughtful, grateful, beautiful, successful, helpful, useful, doubtful.

Doubtless, needless, unless, powerless, helpless, worthless.

Reading and Writing Practice

163. Transcription Word Study

> **fleet** A number of cars operated by the same individual or company.

two-way radio   A radio that both receives and sends messages.

trailer   A vehicle without a motor, designed to be attached to a truck or a car and hauled or pulled.

164.

(shorthand outlines)

(83)

165.

(shorthand outlines)

, apposition

, as clause
; because of comma

(124)

166.

, if clause
autos

two-way
  hyphenated
  before noun

, when clause
contact

, conjunction
engage

(115)

167.

, introductory

territory
; no conjunction

, apposition
advise
whether

, as clause
. courteous
    request

168. (124)

pickup
, as clause

Transcribe:
January 15

147

(131)

Transcription Quiz. For you to supply: 5 commas – 5 commas series; 2 semicolons no conjunction; 2 missing words.

169.

(152)

▶ **Warmup.** Your warmup for the last time is letter No. 142, page 130. Copy the entire letter as many times as you can and as rapidly as you can.

170. Vocabulary Builder

Ng

Omission of Ow

Def, etc.

Gent, Pent

Ring, spring, bring, single, young, wrong, strong.
Brown, down, town, found, round, around, ground, sound.
Definite, defect, defective, develop, divide, differ, different.
Gentle, urgent, spent, expenditure, depend, happened, carpenter.

Reading and Writing Practice

171. Transcription Word Study. *Brake, break.* Both these words occur in the Reading and Writing Practice. Watch out for them.

brake The mechanical device that stops a car.

[shorthand symbols]

He could not stop his car because his brakes did not work.

break   To become disabled.

[shorthand symbols]

If your car should break down, you will be in difficulty.

172.

brakes
, as clause

[shorthand symbols]

dependable
checkup

[shorthand symbols]

; because of comma
, if clause
adjustments

[shorthand symbols]

peace
knowledge
emergency

[shorthand symbols]

(124)

173. [shorthand outlines]

, apposition
Transcribe:
 April 15

[shorthand outlines]

15

[shorthand outlines]

, series
Transcribe:
 $10

[shorthand outlines]

3/

[shorthand outlines]

; no conjunction
attendant

[shorthand outlines]

; no conjunction
commuting

[shorthand outlines] **(121)**

174. [shorthand outlines]

, introductory
approaching
break

[shorthand outlines]

, if clause
first-class
 hyphenated
 before noun

[shorthand outlines] **(60)**

A businessman hires a secretary because he needs someone to take care of office details while he gives his attention to the problems of running a business. When his secretary is in the office, he expects her to do the job for which she has been hired and not spend office time in discussing her personal affairs.

The young lady who is the subject of the following article will have to realize this fact if she is ever to become a secretary.

175. The Office "Visitor"

(280)

Check List

1. Why did one businessman complain about the activities of his substitute secretary?

2. What effect did the substitute's "visiting" have on the work of the other girls in the office?

3. Instead of tending to business, what did the substitute constantly talk about?

Aviation

On December 17, 1903, the good citizens of Kitty Hawk, North Carolina, rubbed their eyes in disbelief. They were sure they saw, off in the distance, something that looked like a big flying box. What they were witnessing, of course, was the birth of a great industry — aviation. That "flying box" was the Wright brothers' plane, which on that day made four successful flights, one for a duration of 59 seconds at a speed of 30 miles an hour.

That flying box was the great, great, granddaddy of today's majestic airliner, which carries 60 passengers from New York to Los Angeles nonstop at a speed of more than 360 miles an hour — with all the comforts of a fine hotel.

In those early days, only the bold and adventurous had the courage to fly in the "flying boxes"; today millions of people fly every year — even the most timid — for air travel is safer than riding in an automobile.

Even though the aviation industry has made almost unbelievable progress since the Wrights built their plane, it is still in its infancy; and we can expect to see some wonderful advances in aviation in the days ahead.

The letters in this chapter deal with various phases of the aviation industry. They are typical of the letters you would take from dictation should you obtain a stenographic position in some branch of that industry.

26

176. Phrase Builder. The following list contains 50 phrases that are frequently used in business letters. Can you read the entire list in 1 minute or less?

If

In

Is

It

If it, if it is, if necessary, if not, if so, if the, if there are, if there is, if we, if this, if you, if you are, if you can, if you could, if you desire, if you do, if you do not, if you have, if you will.

In addition to the, in case, in fact, in his, in its, in order, in order that, in our, in regard, in spite, in that, in the, in this, in this matter, in time, in which.

Is it, is made, is not, is that, is the, is this, is to be, is that the.

It has been, it is, it is the, it was, it will, it will be, it will not be.

► **Warmup Phrase Letter.** The following 138-word letter contains 33 frequently used phrases. Be sure to read the letter before making a copy of it.

177.

[shorthand outlines]

(138)

Reading and Writing Practice

178. Transcription Word Study

courtesy flight A flight at no expense to the passenger.

DC-7 A powerful Douglas-made plane that carries 60 passengers at a cruising speed of 365 miles an hour.

179.

[shorthand outlines]

flights
, if clause
; no conjunction

[shorthand outlines]

; because of comma
, parenthetical
mind

[shorthand outlines]

, series
, when clause
strength

[shorthand outlines]

dc=7

[shorthand outlines]

accept
. courteous
  request

(148)

180.

, apposition

[shorthand outlines]

first-class
hyphenated
before noun

; because of comma
, introductory
travelers

10

, parenthetical
; no conjunction
preparing

1940

(144)

181.

, parenthetical
discussing
Kansas City

15

shorthand outlines

, if clause
accommodations

(106)

Transcription Quiz. For you to supply: 6 commas — 2 commas series, 1 comma *when* clause, 1 comma introductory, 1 comma conjunction, 1 comma *if* clause; 1 semicolon no conjunction; 2 missing words.

182.

shorthand outlines

161

16

66

(147)

159

LESSON
27

▶ **Warmup.** Read the first paragraph of letter No. 177 on page 156. Then copy that paragraph as many times as you can and as rapidly as you can before your teacher begins the regular class work.

183. Brief-Form Chart. The following chart contains 48 brief forms and derivatives. Can you read the entire chart in less than 1 minute?

1. Company-keep, accompany, accompanied, companies-keeps, unaccompanied, accompaniment.
2. Conclude, conclusion, conclusive, concluded, inconclusive, concludes.
3. Progress, progressed, progresses, progressive, progressiveness, progressively.
4. Order, ordered, ordering, reorder, disorder, orderly.
5. Stand, standing, understand, withstand, notwithstanding, misunderstand.
6. Satisfy-satisfactory, satisfaction, dissatisfied, dissatisfaction, unsatisfactory, satisfactorily.
7. Letter-let, letters, lettering-letting, booklet, leaflet, pamphlet.
8. Allow, allows, allowed, allowance, allowable, disallow.

184. Geographical Expressions

Minneapolis, St. Paul, Memphis, Dayton, Rochester, Houston, Fort Worth.

Maine, New York, Missouri, Texas, Massachusetts, Oklahoma, Michigan.

Reading and Writing Practice

185. Transcription Word Study

take-off The rising of a plane from the ground.

low ceiling Dense clouds, fog, or smog close to the ground. The lower the ceiling, the more difficult it is for planes to take off and land.

surface transportation Trains and buses.

186.

, apposition
Transcribe:
May 17
, as clause
agency

E. 9. (132)

, *as* clause
accompany

(132)

187.

; *because of* comma
, *parenthetical*
take-offs

flown
millions
, *conjunction*

seven-hour
hyphenated
before noun
, *conjunction*

(119)

188.

tiresome
traveling
, *conjunction*

Houston
modern

, introductory

won't
. courteous
request

(125)

189.

encountered
Transcribe:
June 17

, when clause
beyond

, conjunction
inconvenience

frequent
, conjunction

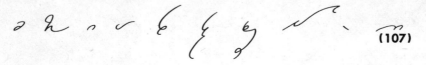

(107)

Transcription Quiz. For you to supply: 5 commas — 2 commas conjunction, 2 commas series, 1 comma introductory; 2 semicolons no conjunction; 2 missing words.

190.

[shorthand outlines]

(151)

▶ **Warmup.** For your warmup, use the second paragraph of letter No. 177 on page 156. Copy it slowly, then rapidly, and finally in your best shorthand.

191. Word Families

-age

-bility

-cate

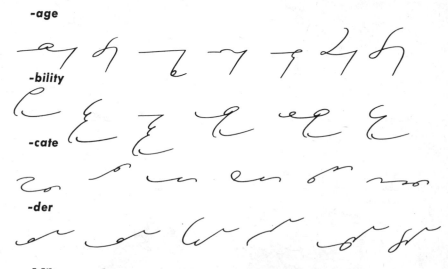

-der

Mileage, package, manager, encourage, message, village, baggage.
Ability, possibility, impossibility, liability, reliability, probability.
Complicate, indicate, locate, allocate, educate, communicate.
Reader, leader, broader, tender, louder, powder.

Reading and Writing Practice

192. Transcription Word Study

complicated Difficult to understand.

threatening weather Cloudy or windy weather that usually indicates a rain storm or a snow storm.

economy Thriftiness.

in all probability Doubtless.

193. *[shorthand outlines]*

, parenthetical
pilots
assemblies

possess
, conjunction

worth while
  no noun,
  no hyphen
, if clause

. courteous
  request

(138)

194. *[shorthand outlines]*

, introductory

166

; no conjunction
installments
furniture

routine
, apposition

, when clause
notified

advantage
. courteous
request

(145)

195.

, series
luncheon

; because of comma
, introductory

, as clause
; no conjunction

, parenthetical
, introductory
practical

(122)

196.

, parenthetical
threatening
flying

traveling
, if clause

, when clause
probability
clouds

out-of-town
  hyphenated
  before noun
, introductory

(shorthand symbols) **(142)**

Transcription Quiz. For you to supply: 7 commas—1 comma *if* clause, 1 comma introductory, 4 commas series, 1 comma *when* clause; 1 semicolon no conjunction; 2 missing words.

197.

(shorthand outlines)

(143)

LESSON

29

► **Warmup.** For your warmup, use the third paragraph of letter No. 177 on page 156. Copy the paragraph slowly, then rapidly, and finally in your best shorthand.

198. Word Beginnings and Endings

Al-

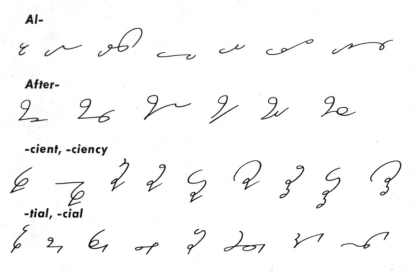

After-

-cient, -ciency

-tial, -cial

Also, alter, alternative, almost, although, already, altogether.
Afternoon, aftermath, after-dinner, afterward, afterthought, aftercare.
Patient, impatient, sufficient, efficient, proficient, deficient, efficiency, proficiency, deficiency.
Special, essential, partial, initial, official, financial, substantial, credential.

Reading and Writing Practice

199. Transcription Word Study

    ascends Goes up.

descends Comes down.

deplane Leave the plane.

200.
, apposition
Transcribe:
March 21

, parenthetical
crowded

, introductory
; because of comma
entitle

, introductory
annoyed

, if clause
altered

efficiency
, introductory

(172)

201.

(104)

, introductory
essential

postage-paid
hyphenated
before noun

———
assembled
, introductory

202.
announcing
, series
, apposition

Homework Check List

When you do each day's homework, do you get the most out of the time you spend on it by

1. Reading the Transcription Word Studies before you begin on the Reading and Writing Practice?

2. Reading all shorthand aloud before making a copy of it?

ascends
descends

experience
deplane

; no conjunction
minutes'

(133)

203.

partial
, conjunction

recognition
, introductory

initial
, as clause

, when clause
personally

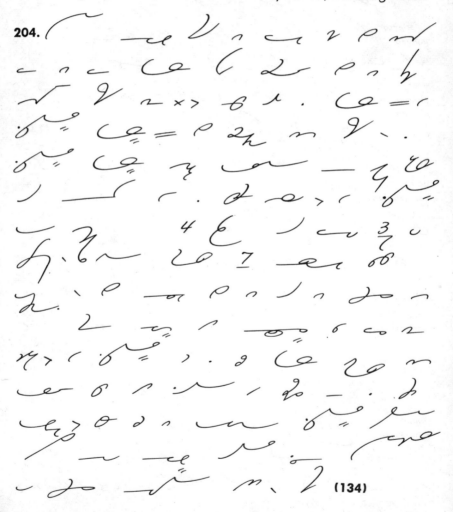

(133)

Transcription Quiz. For you to supply: 4 commas — 2 commas series, 2 commas parenthetical; 1 semicolon no conjunction; 2 missing words.

204.

(134)

▶ **Warmup.** Copy letter No. 177 on page 156 as rapidly as you can. If there is time, copy it again in your very best shorthand.

205. Vocabulary Builder

Oo

Ĭa, Ea

Th

Ses

Noon, flew, food, routine, grew, group, cool.
Appreciate, aviation, associate, brilliant, appropriate, piano, area, create.
Thursday, though, thrill, thoughtful, smooth, thousands, beneath.
Services, arises, realizes, addresses, releases, system, access.

Reading and Writing Practice

206. Transcription Word Study

en route   On the way.

hangar   A shed for housing planes.

207.

[shorthand outlines]

; because of comma
, apposition

[shorthand outlines]

hangar
appropriate

[shorthand outlines]

, introductory
en route

[shorthand outlines]

; because of comma
, introductory

[shorthand outlines]

, conjunction
appreciate

[shorthand outlines]

(178)

208.
, as clause
realizes

34

650

40

; no conjunction
distance

nation's
; no conjunction

(100)

209.
; no conjunction
, parenthetical
hesitate

husband's
; no conjunction

arises
, when clause

(88)

Secretarial Pointer

One of the first things you must learn is to follow instructions. There will be times when you think that the instructions you have been given are wrong; but that does not entitle you to ignore or change them. In the following story, Julia Smith almost came to grief when she received instructions that were contrary to what she had been taught in school.

210. To Tidy or Not To Tidy

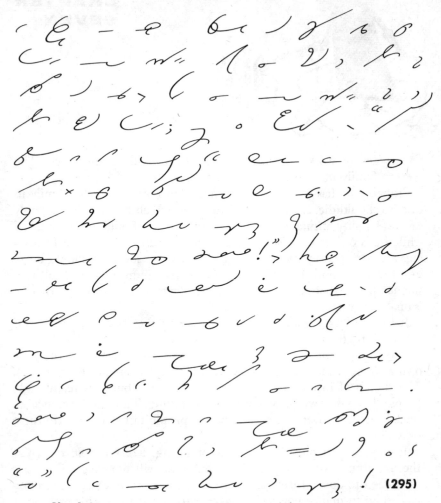

(295)

Check List

1. How was Mr. Wood different from most business-men in the way he kept his desk?

2. What instructions did Julia disregard that made her employer angry?

3. What lesson did Julia learn as a result of this incident?

CHAPTER SEVEN

Insurance

Nearly every working person carries some kind of insurance. The average family man is insured against many kinds of losses.

Probably he has a life insurance policy to take care of his family in case he should die. If he owns the house in which he lives, he probably carries liability insurance in case some visitor should injure himself while he is on the premises; fire insurance in case the house or furnishings are damaged by fire; theft insurance in case someone should break into the house and steal valuable possessions. He may have a health insurance policy that provides for monthly payments in the event that he is unable to work.

If the family owns a dog, they may have a policy that pays the bills if the dog bites the mailman or the deliveryman!

Owning insurance is as natural as owning a car. Nearly everything we own may be insured against loss — our property, our health, our lives. The theory of insurance may seem complicated, but it is really quite simple. It boils down to two words: risk sharing. Through insurance we spread our risks over a large number of people rather than carry these risks alone.

Insurance also provides a means of saving. Most people recognize the importance of saving regularly, but they will not save unless they are forced to do so. Insurance forces a person to save. Once he has purchased an insurance policy, he makes every effort to pay his premiums; he knows that, if he misses a payment, he may lose his entire investment.

The insurance business, touching as it does the lives of all of us, employs many thousands of office workers, none of whom are more important than the stenographers and secretaries. If you were a stenographer in an insurance executive's office, your dictation might be similar to that of the letters in this chapter.

211. Phrase Builder. The following list contains 43 useful business-letter phrases. How fast can you read through the entire list? To help you master these phrases so that you can write them without hesitation, many of them are used in the Reading and Writing Practice of this lesson.

Many

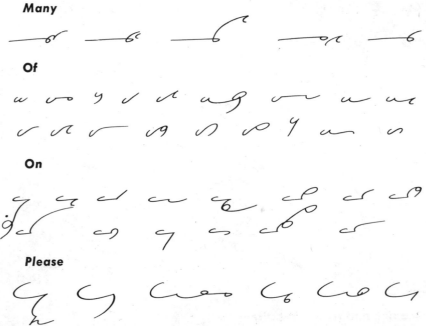

Of

On

Please

Many other, many things, many times, many thousands, many of the.
Of all, of any, of his, of it, of its, of life, of Mr., of our, of ours, of the, of those, of them, of these, of this, of that, of which, of work, of you.
On behalf, on his, on it, on our, on sale, on that, on the, on these, on time, on us, on which, on your, on that day, on them.
Please be sure, please have, please let me, please see, please write, please ship.

212.

[shorthand outlines]

(144)

Reading and Writing Practice

213. Transcription Word Study

lapse *(verb)* To be no longer in effect.

premium The amount paid an insurance company at regular intervals to keep an insurance policy in force.

214.

, as clause
purchase

surprise
, parenthetical

, Introductory
; because of comma
believe

keenly
aware

(144)

215.

Transcribe:
May 5

reason
, conjunction

(142)

216.

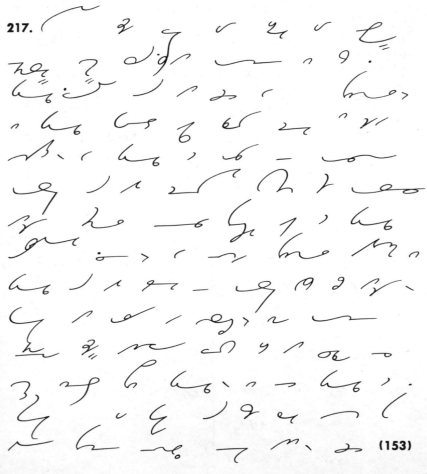

, when clause

(124)

Transcription Quiz. For you to supply: 5 commas — 1 comma introductory, 1 comma conjunction, 2 commas parenthetical, 1 comma as clause; 1 semicolon because of comma; 2 missing words.

217.

(153)

LESSON 32

▶ **Warmup.** Your warmup letter is No. 212 on page 182.

Today, let us use a slightly different plan for warming up.

Instead of working with a complete paragraph, let us develop speed on individual sentences. Let us break each sentence into several parts and practice each part separately. For example, this is the way you would practice the first sentence in letter 212:

1. Write slowly in your best shorthand the group of words *Dear Mr. Bass: May I ask you.*

2. Write the same group of words two or three times more, trying to increase your writing speed each time.

3. Follow steps 1 and 2 with the next group of words *to do me a favor.*

4. Finally, write the complete sentence in shorthand.

Follow this procedure with as many sentences in the first paragraph of letter No. 212 as time permits.

Your warmup should look like this in your shorthand notebook.

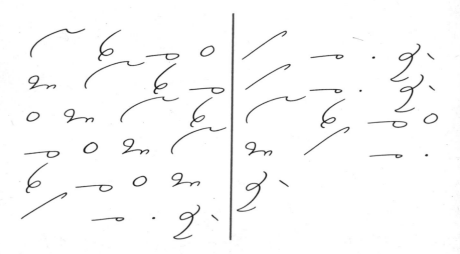

218. Brief-Form Chart. In the following chart there are 48 brief forms and derivatives. Can you read the entire chart in 1 minute or less?

1. Correspond-correspondence, corresponding, correspondent, corresponds, correspondingly, corresponded.
2. Advertise, advertiser, advertisement, advertising, advertised, unadvertised.
3. Present-presence, presentation, represent, representative, presented, presents.
4. State, statements, misstate, reinstate, stateroom, stately.
5. Consider, considerate, considers, considerable, unconsidered, considering.
6. Part, partner, depart, impart, parted, parts.
7. Ever, whenever, wherever, whatever, whichever, however.
8. Body, bodies, embodies, everybody, somebody, nobody.

219. Geographical Expressions

Birmingham, Spokane, Tacoma, Charlotte, Albany, Worcester.
Idaho, New Hampshire, North Carolina, North Dakota, Washington, Alabama, Arizona.

220. Transcription Word Study

primarily   In the first place, originally, mainly.

liability insurance   Insurance that pays for any damage or injury that the insured person may cause to another person or his property.

221.

accident
, apposition

; because of comma
, introductory
recommendation

primarily
, parenthetical
, introductory

advise
. courteous
*   request*

(164)

222. *[shorthand outline]*

liability
occurred *[shorthand outline]*

24-page
  hyphenated
  before noun
; no conjunction   24= *[shorthand outline]*

, introductory
relatives *[shorthand outline]*

(94)

223. *[shorthand outline]*

, introductory
enclosed *[shorthand outline]*

, series
self-addressed *[shorthand outline]*

, as clause
entitled
year's *[shorthand outline]* 75

(94)

Transcription Quiz. For you to supply: 5 commas—1 comma as clause, 2 commas series, 1 comma *if* clause, 1 comma *when* clause; 1 semicolon no conjunction; 2 missing words.

224.

(167)

▶ **Warmup.** Your warmup letter is No. 212 on page 182. Follow the same warmup procedure on the sentences in paragraph 2 that you used for the sentences in paragraph 1 of letter 212. Remember, try to increase your writing speed with each repetition.

225. Word Families

Rec-

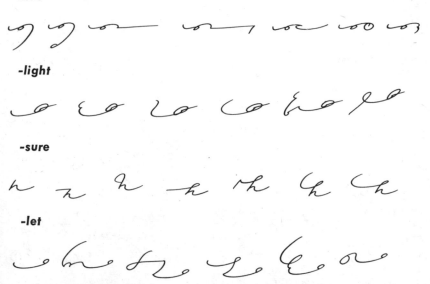

-light

-sure

-let

Recover, recovery, recommend, recommendation, recall, require, reconsider.
Light, slight, flight, plight, spotlight, daylight.
Sure, insure, assure, measure, treasure, pressure, pleasure.
Let, booklet, pamphlet, leaflet, bracelet, outlet.

Reading and Writing Practice

226. Transcription Word Study

option   Choice.

mature   To run to the limit of its time.

227. [shorthand symbols]

Transcribe:
$40,000   [shorthand symbols]

, introductory
; no conjunction
piece   [shorthand symbols]

, parenthetical
; because of comma
minds   [shorthand symbols]

, conjunction
accepted   [shorthand symbols]

, when clause
, series
personally   [shorthand symbols]

, parenthetical   [shorthand symbols]

(139)

228. [shorthand symbols]

various
described
, parenthetical

, introductory
benefit

(105)

229.
, as clause
20-payment
   hyphenated
   before noun

20=   21.

, apposition
, introductory
, parenthetical

, if clause
local

, parenthetical
obligation

pleasure
; because of comma

193

, if clause [shorthand outlines] **(136)**

230. [shorthand outlines]

; no conjunction
, conjunction [shorthand outlines]

, conjunction
student's [shorthand outlines]

premium
Transcribe: [shorthand outlines] 18/ . [shorthand] 15/
$18

, if clause
touch [shorthand outlines] **(134)**

231. [shorthand outlines]

, parenthetical [shorthand outlines]

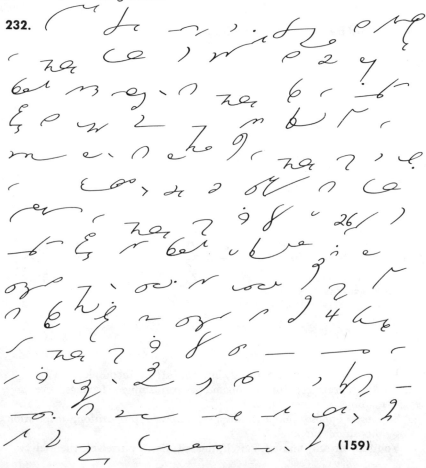

(77)

Transcription Quiz. For you to supply: 7 commas — 4 commas parenthetical, 2 commas introductory, 1 comma *if* clause; 1 semicolon because
of comma; 2 missing words.

232.

(159)

▶ **Warmup.** Your warmup letter is No. 212 on page 182.

For today, take the sentences in paragraph 3 of the letter and follow the steps outlined on page 186. Practice each sentence in two or three parts.

233. Word Beginnings and Endings

In-

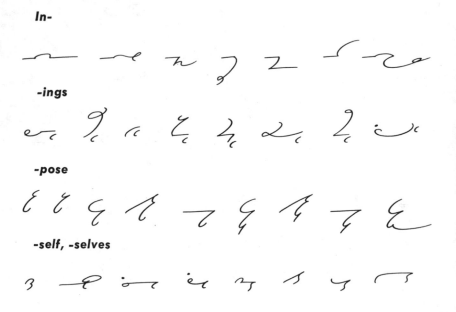

-ings

-pose

-self, -selves

Income, increase, insure, invest, inform, intend, incomplete.

Earnings, savings, things, openings, furnishings, feelings, evenings, holdings.

Suppose, oppose, propose, dispose, impose, proposition, disposition, imposition, proposal.

Yourself, myself, himself, herself, oneself, itself, ourselves, themselves.

Reading and Writing Practice

234. Transcription Word Study

breadwinner The one who supports a family.

cancellation Wiping out, annulling.

235. *(shorthand outlines)*

, series
. courteous
  request

, parenthetical
mornings

, parenthetical
Governor

well-known
  hyphenated
  before noun
, conjunction
worth while
  no noun,
  no hyphen

(134)

236.

breadwinner's

, parenthetical
; no conjunction
thrift

families
, as clause

, if clause
won't

whether
. courteous
request

(137)

237.

, when clause
providing

, series

, parenthetical
, introductory
hearts

198

standard
forward

. courteous
request
coupon

(125)

238.

directors
, parenthetical
; because of comma

1940

, apposition
territory

, if clause
Hartford

, parenthetical
incidentally

(118)

239.
, introductory
debt
company's

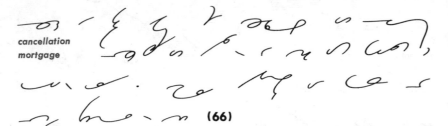

cancellation
mortgage

(66)

Transcription Quiz. For you to supply: 7 commas—1 comma *if* clause, 2 commas conjunction, 2 commas series, 2 commas parenthetical; 1 semicolon because of comma; 2 missing words.

240.

(135)

▶ **Warmup.** For the last time your warmup letter will be No. 212 on page 182.

Break the postscript into two or three parts and practice each part separately as outlined on page 186.

241. Vocabulary Builder

Omission of T

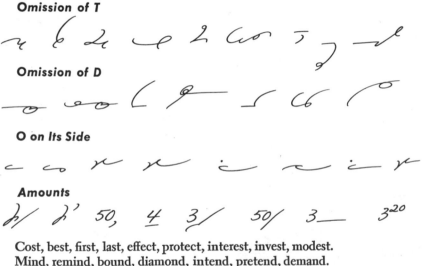

Omission of D

O on Its Side

Amounts

Cost, best, first, last, effect, protect, interest, invest, modest.
Mind, remind, bound, diamond, intend, pretend, demand.
On, only, store, stole, whole, call, home, stone.
Few dollars; few cents; 50 per cent; 400; $3,000; $50; 3,000,000; $3.20.

Reading and Writing Practice

242. Transcription Word Study

    theft insurance Insurance that provides protection against loss from the stealing of personal property.

underinsured Not carrying sufficient protection against loss.

inventory A list of the things that a person owns, usually showing the value of each item.

243.

[Shorthand content]

, as clause
strangers

soul
, introductory

, as clause
familiar

unusual
, when clause

, introductory
; because of comma
theft

suffering
; no conjunction

(164)

244.

, if clause
awakened

2:30

, introductory
, series

Transcribe:
  $3,000
, conjunction

underinsured
, parenthetical

peace
, introductory

(139)

Good businessmen soon learn who are the producers on their staff and who are the "drones." Though they may say nothing, employers know which employees are giving "full measure" during office hours and which ones are doing only as much as they have to.

Often the first inkling of this fact comes to employees when there are promotions to be made or when someone has to be let out. The conscientious employees are always the first to be promoted and the last to be let out.

Frank Meade found this out, as you will learn from the following story.

245. Good Work Habits Win Promotion

[Shorthand text]

(278)

Check List

1. What did Frank notice about the work habits of some of his co-workers?

2. How were the working habits of these employees different from his?

3. How was Frank rewarded for his good work habits?

CHAPTER Eight

Banking

Most people look upon a bank as a safe place in which to keep their money. True, there is no safer place in which to keep your money. Not only is your money safe in a bank, but it can also work for you while it is there — by earning interest.

A bank offers many services other than "safekeeping" — services without which business could not operate effectively. Here are a few ways in which banks serve us:

> If you want to build a house, your bank lends money for this purpose.
>
> If you want to start in business for yourself, your bank may grant a business loan.
>
> If you want to buy a car but cannot pay cash for it, your bank may offer a personal loan.
>
> If you want a safe place in which to store valuable papers, such as insurance policies, government bonds, etc., the safe-deposit department of your bank offers storage facilities.

Every person, no matter how modest his income, should have a banker — just as he has a doctor or a lawyer. The banker can be a real friend in need when financial problems arise.

Today's bank is a friendly place. Banks have only one thing to sell — service — and customers are made to feel as much "at home." as if they were in their favorite department store. If you were to talk to some of the people who work in the bank, you would find that their work is interesting and varied. Banks carry on a great deal of business by correspondence, and the stenographer and the secretary play important roles in the daily affairs of the business. The letters in this chapter are typical of those that might be dictated to you in a banking office.

246. Phrase Builder. The following list contains 41 frequently used phrases. Can you read the list in less than a minute?

They can, they wouldn't, they have, they may be, they will, they will be, they will have.

This information, this is, this is the, this letter, this matter, this might, this may, this means, this month, this morning, this time, this will.

To collect, to carry, to consider, to cover, to enclose, to get, to give, to go, to his, to it, to keep, to talk, to tell, to the, to their, to them, to these, to think, to this, to those, to you, to that.

▶ **Warmup Phrase Letter.** The following 147-word letter, which is your warmup for this chapter, contains 38 phrases. How fast can you read and copy the letter?

247. *[shorthand]* **(147)**

Reading and Writing Practice

248. Transcription Word Study

safe-deposit box A compartment in a vault for the storage and protection of valuables.

income and outgo The money that you make and the money that you spend.

249. *[shorthand]*

, introductory
; because of comma
worried

out-of-the-way
  hyphenated
  before noun

month's

. courteous
  request

canceled
, *as* clause
; because of comma

, *if* clause
balance

(139)

250.

bank's
, conjunction

growth
, parenthetical
; because of comma

(137)

; no conjunction
mutual

wherever
, series
, introductory

251.
, apposition
drive-in
  hyphenated
  before noun

Transcribe:
  22 Street
, series

require
, when clause

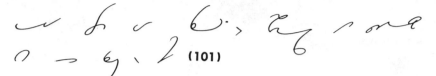

(101)

Transcription Quiz. For you to supply: 4 commas — 1 comma conjunction, 2 commas apposition, 1 comma parenthetical; 1 semicolon no conjunction; 2 missing words.

252.

(144)

▶ **Warmup.** Your warmup letter is No. 247 on page 208. Warmup on the sentence in paragraph 1, breaking down the sentence into two or three convenient parts. Write each part of the sentence three or four times, trying to write faster with each repetition. After you have practiced a sentence in this way, write the entire sentence once in your best shorthand.

253. Brief-Form Chart. There are 42 brief forms and derivatives in this chart. Can you read the chart as rapidly from bottom to top as you can from top to bottom?

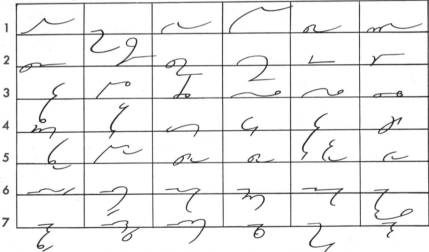

1. Endless, nevertheless, thankless, timeless, useless, worthless.
2. Acknowledgment, advertisement, accompaniment, government, shipment, statement.
3. Publicly, directly, generally, gladly, greatly, immediately.
4. Succession, objection, organization, presentation, publication, satisfaction.
5. Believer, director, outer, user, speaker, thinker.
6. Uncorrected, uncovered, unworkable, unsuccessful, unimportant, unbusinesslike.
7. Inexperienced, inconsiderate, inconclusive, inside, invaluable, instances.

254. Geographical Expressions

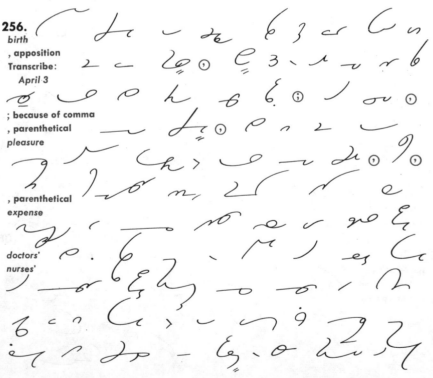

Springfield, Greenfield, Garfield, Plainfield, Westfield, Bloomfield.
Massachusetts, Kansas, Illinois, New Jersey, California, Delaware.

Reading and Writing Practice

255. Transcription Word Study

public-opinion poll An expression by a group of people
of their feelings or opinions about a subject.

long-term loan A loan that usually runs for two years
or longer.

256.
birth
, apposition
Transcribe:
April 3

; because of comma
, parenthetical
pleasure

, parenthetical
expense

doctors'
nurses'

213

low-cost
   hyphenated
   before noun
  , conjunction

low cost
   no noun,
   no hyphen

(134)

257.
public-opinion
   hyphenated
   before noun

, series
promptly .

furthermore
, introductory

, conjunction
enclosed

(108)

258.
personal-loan
   hyphenated
   before noun

214

, parenthetical
Transcribe:
$3

12

inconvenient
, if clause

4:30

, if clause
; no conjunction
transaction

, as clause
welcome

(146)

259.

, if clause
probably

elsewhere
, when clause
, if clause

215

, if clause
, apposition
treasurer

(121)

Transcription Quiz. For you to supply: 6 commas—2 commas *if* clause, 2 commas series, 1 comma introductory, 1 comma as clause; 2 semicolons—1 semicolon because of comma, 1 semicolon no conjunction; 2 missing words.

260.

(124)

▶ **Warmup.** For your warmup today, practice on the sentences in paragraph 2 of letter No. 247 on page 208. Break down each sentence into as many parts as you feel desirable.

261. Word Families

-side

Ind-

-son

Book

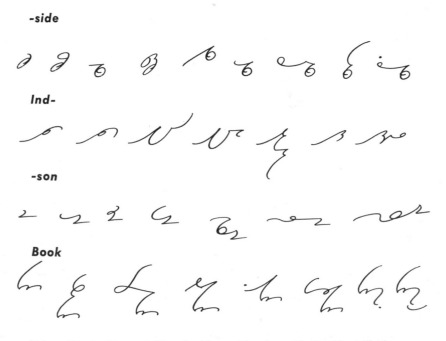

Side, aside, inside, outside, decide, reside, alongside, beside, hillside.

Indicate, indication, independent, independence, indispensable, induce, industry.

Son, reason, season, person, comparison, crimson, grandson.

Book, passbook, bankbook, textbook, handbook, pocketbook, book-keeping, bookkeeper.

Reading and Writing Practice

262. Transcription Word Study

passbook A depositor's book in which the bank records deposits and withdrawals. It is also called a bankbook.

indispensable Essential, necessary.

sizable Big.

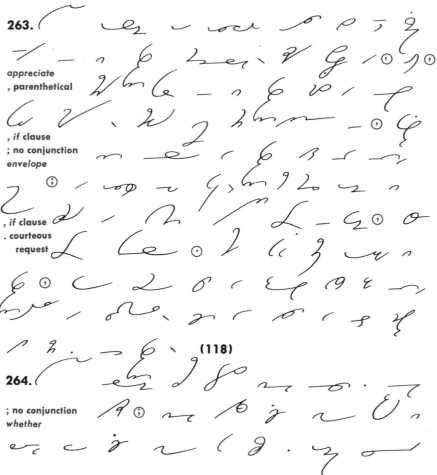

263.

appreciate
, parenthetical

, if clause
; no conjunction
envelope

, if clause
. courteous
request

(118)

264.

; no conjunction
whether

; because of comma
, series
until

, when clause
independence

, conjunction
indispensable

(121)

265.

, as clause
besides

70,

recommendations
indicates

hesitation
, introductory

, parenthetical

, conjunction
beginning

(134)

266.

, introductory
, parenthetical
embarrassing

. courteous
request
, conjunction

, conjunction
compounded

(120)

267.

, if clause
boy's

Transcription Quiz. For you to supply: 5 commas — 2 commas parenthetical, 2 commas introductory, 1 comma *if* clause; 1 semicolon because of comma; 2 missing words.

268.

. **courteous**
request

(138)

LESSON
39

▶ **Warmup.** Today, warm up on the sentences in paragraph 3 of letter No. 247 on page 208. To be on the safe side, why not turn to page 186 and reread the instructions for warming up.

269. Word Beginnings and Endings

-ulate, -ulation

-fication

Super-, Supr-

Incl-

Congratulate, regulate, stimulate, populate, congratulations, stimulation.

Identification, justification, classification, modification, notification, qualifications, specifications.

Supervise, superficial, supervisor, superior, supreme, support, supported, superhuman.

Incline, inclines, inclined, inclination, include, includes, including, included.

Reading and Writing Practice

270. Transcription Word Study

identification card A card bearing a person's name and
address and other identifying information. Usually, the
card bears the owner's signature.

the twenties The years 1920 through 1929.

cordial Warm, friendly.

271.

, introductory
identification
similar

employee
, parenthetical

discussed
, conjunction

co-operate
devise
, parenthetical

(132)

272.

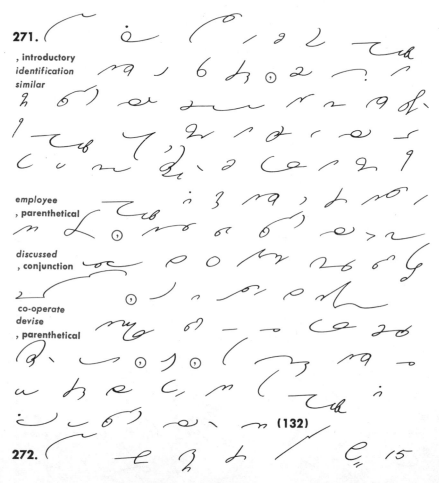

; no conjunction
reminder

, parenthetical
; because of comma
delighted

, introductory

(114)

273. 40

depositors
growth

, series 20's 30's 40's

, conjunction

Transcription Check List

Remember, you can never become an efficient stenographer unless you can spell and punctuate correctly; therefore, be sure that you

1. Know the reason for the use of each punctuation mark in your Reading and Writing Practice.

2. Look in the margin of your shorthand page for the reason for the use of a punctuation mark if there is any doubt in your mind.

3. Spell aloud at least once each word in the margin.

, as clause
anniversary

(139)

274.
, apposition
Transcribe:
October 4

, as clause
possession

, if clause
already

anxious
, conjunction

225

(112)

Transcription Quiz. For you to supply: 6 commas — 2 commas conjunction, 2 commas parenthetical, 1 comma *when* clause, 1 comma introductory; 1 semicolon no conjunction; 2 missing words.

275.

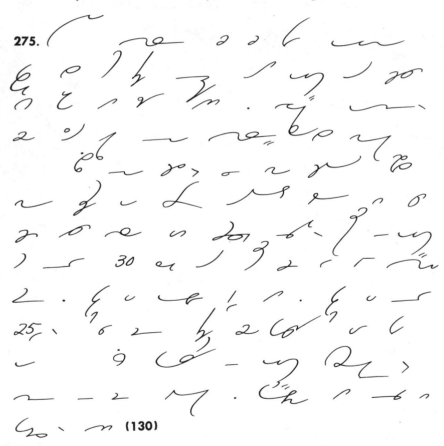

(130)

▶ **Warmup.** For the last time, your warmup letter will be No. 247 on page 208. Warm up in the same way that you did in the preceding lessons of this chapter.

276. Vocabulary Builder

Abbreviated Words

Tern, Term, Dern

Intersection

Den

Convenience-convenient, inconvenience-inconvenient, privilege, memo-randum, significance-significant, reluctance-reluctant.

Turn, stern, attorney, eastern, western, term, termed, determine, modern.

A.m., p.m., Chamber of Commerce, C.O.D.

Sudden, evidence, accident, guidance, danger, abandon, student.

Reading and Writing Practice

277. Transcription Word Study

   estate A person's property and possessions.

executor The person appointed by the maker of a will to carry out the terms of the will.

chronic Continuing for a long time; continuous.

278.

executor
, series

attorney
, conjunction
, when clause

(110)

279.
income-tax
hyphenated
before noun
, as clause

questions
, series
, introductory

, introductory
judgment
practical

appointment
, introductory
, if clause

, apposition — 4-5321

(140)

280.
companies
volume
Canada

(104)

Secretarial Pointer

Every employer wants the people who work for him to be contented and happy, and he does all he can to provide as ideal working conditions for his staff as possible. Occasionally, however, an employee will have a real grievance; and when he does, the employer wants to hear about it.

But no employer likes to have a chronic complainer on his staff, especially one who complains about little things about which nothing can usually be done. When he finds such a person on his staff, the employer loses no time replacing him, as Ethel learns in the story that follows.

281. Chronic Complainers Not Welcome

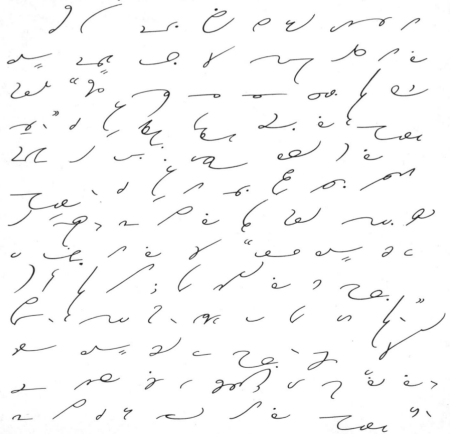

(275)

Check List

1. What jobs was Ethel Smith constantly complaining about?
2. What advice did Ethel's best friend give her?
3. What important lesson did Ethel have to learn?

CHAPTER Nine

Advertising

Ralph Waldo Emerson has been credited with the saying that, if a person builds a better mousetrap than his neighbor, the world will beat a path to his door. Emerson was indeed a great poet and essayist, but we suspect that he would not have been very successful as an advertising man; for what would it avail a man to build the world's best mousetrap if he did not let the world know about it?

After a man builds his mousetrap, he must announce the fact to the mousetrap-buying public; he must set forth the reasons why his mousetrap will catch more mice than the mousetraps already on the market; he must let the public know where they can buy the mousetrap and how much it costs. In short, even the world's best mousetrap must be advertised — and that is the function of the advertising industry.

Advertising in America goes hand in hand with our system of business. In order to produce goods in large quantities, we must have means of letting the people know that the merchandise is available. Advertising uses various media — newspapers, magazines, radio, television, billboards — even skywriting! Sometimes we may think we are exposed to too much advertising, but we must remember that advertising enables us to have good television programs at no cost to us; and it keeps down the cost of newspapers and magazines. More important, however, is that advertising enables us to enjoy more goods and services at less cost than would otherwise be possible.

Working in an advertising department or in an advertising agency can be among the most interesting and exciting of all office jobs. The letters in this chapter may give you some insight into what it is like working in this lively field of advertising.

282. Phrase Builder. The following list contains 43 frequently used business-letter phrases. It should not take you more than a minute to read through the list.

Very

We

Which

Who

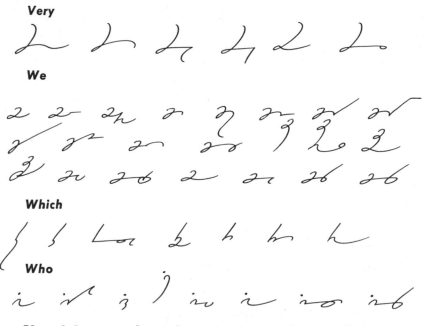

Very glad, very good, very important, very much, very well, very many.
We are, we are not, we are sure, we can, we can be, we cannot, we could, we could not, we did, we do not, we enclose, we get, we have, we have your letter, we feel, we find, we know, we might, we will, we must, we need, we made.
Which have been, which is, which means, which we are, which you, which you can, which you will.
Who are, who desire, who is, who have, who know, who will, who make, who made.

283.

(104)

Reading and Writing Practice

284. Transcription Word Study

real estate Property in the form of buildings and land.

exclusively Solely; in a restrictive manner.

medium That through which anything is accomplished.

testimonial A statement certifying to the value of something or to the particular accomplishment of a person.

285.

234

, when clause
magazine

well-known
   hyphenated
   before noun
, introductory

, introductory
, parenthetical
traceable

, series
corresponding

286.

, apposition
announcement

attracted
; because of comma

, as clause
; because of comma
exclusively

40/ [shorthand outline]

(93)

287. [shorthand outline]

beginning
, conjunction

[shorthand outlines]

already
; no conjunction
, introductory

[shorthand outlines]

, parenthetical
toward

[shorthand outlines]

Transcribe:
November 15

15. [shorthand outline]

(137)

288. [shorthand outline]

[shorthand outlines]

, when clause
Canadian
budget

[shorthand outlines]

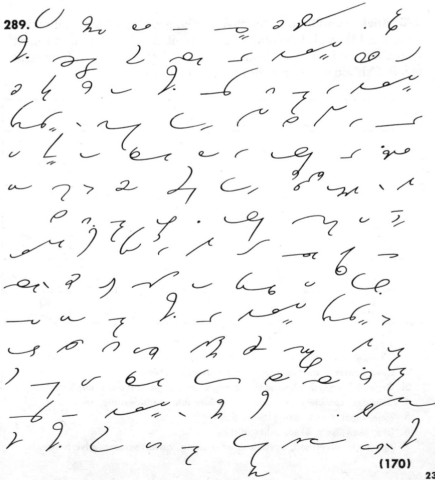

company's
until　　(107)

Transcription Quiz. For you to supply: 5 commas—1 comma as clause, 1 comma apposition, 2 commas parenthetical, 1 comma *if* clause; 2 semicolons—1 semicolon because of comma; 1 semicolon no conjunction; 2 missing words.

289.

(170)

LESSON
42

▶ **Warmup.** Your warmup letter today is No. 283 on page 234. Continue to follow the warmup plan that you used in Chapter 8, breaking each sentence into parts, writing each part several times as rapidly as possible, and finally writing the complete sentence.

290. Brief-Form Chart. This chart contains 42 brief forms and derivatives. Read through the entire chart once; it should not take you more than a minute to do this. Then, go back and read each line from right to left. Can you read the words just as rapidly in this way?

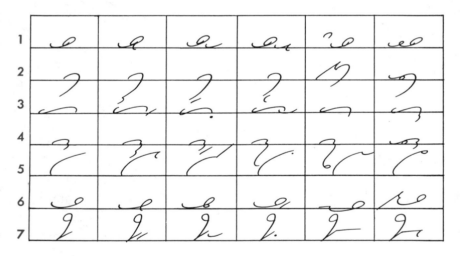

1. Write, writes, writer, writers, underwrite, rewrite.
2. Cover, covers, covered, coverings, discover, recover.
3. Organize, organized, organizing, organizer, organization, organizations.
4. Consider, considers, considered, considerable, considerably, reconsider.
5. Time, times, timed, timing, timer, timely.
6. Like, likes, likely, liked, unlike, dislike.
7. Advertise, advertised, advertiser, advertising, advertisement, advertisements.

291. Geographical Expressions

Pittsburgh, Harrisburg, Plattsburg, Greensburg, Newburg, Fitchburg.
America, American, Canada, Canadian, England, English, United States.

Reading and Writing Practice

292. Transcription Word Study

pattern   A design or model for making things.

clients   Customers.

293.

, apposition

10

fortunate
, introductory
, as clause

quality
, series

; because of comma
won't

. courteous
    request   **(124)**

294.

, introductory
naturally

, parenthetical
, introductory
women

; no conjunction
, introductory
fair

high-quality
   hyphenated
   before noun
, if clause

(167)

295.

, if clause

(shorthand outlines)

, introductory

families
, apposition

buyers
, series

(132)

296.

Company's
, when clause

, introductory
; because of comma
reason

employees
, introductory

well trained

no noun,
no hyphen

, if clause

. courteous
request

(124)

Transcription Quiz. For you to supply: 4 commas—1 comma conjunction, 2 commas introductory, 1 comma *if* clause; 1 semicolon no conjunction; 2 missing words.

297.

(137)

242

▶ **Warmup.** Your warmup letter for today is No. 283 on page 234. Warm up on the sentence in paragraph 2, breaking it down into convenient groups.

298. Word Families

-vision

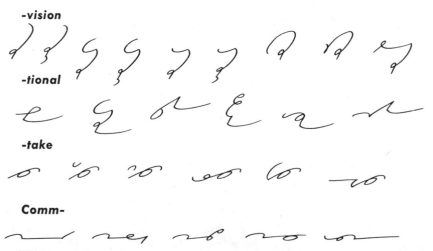

-tional

-take

Comm-

Vision, visions, provision, provisions, revision, revisions, division, subdivision, television.
National, professional, additional, exceptional, occasional, conditional.
Take, overtake, undertake, retake, partake, mistake.
Comment, commercial, committee, command, recommend.

Reading and Writing Practice

299. Transcription Word Study

reprint A second or new printing of a book, article, circular, etc.

pioneers The first ones in a field.

network A chain of radio or television stations.

allotted Set aside for a particular purpose.

300.
received
, as clause
, apposition

[shorthand outlines]

high-grade
  hyphenated
  before noun

[shorthand outlines]

, parenthetical
; because of comma
, when clause

[shorthand outlines]

, conjunction
later

[shorthand outlines] **(146)**

301.
two-page
  hyphenated
  before noun

[shorthand outlines]

244

, series
, as clause
colors
, introductory

receive
; no conjunction

, if clause
overlook
, introductory
well written
   no noun,
   no hyphen

, as clause
comments

(154)

302.

director
Green's

, introductory
connected

well-known
hyphenated
before noun

; because of comma
, parenthetical

(140)

303.

, introductory
assistant
experience

; because of comma
, if clause
handicap

, as clause
exceptional —
courses

(shorthand symbols) **(134)**

Transcription Quiz. For you to supply: 4 commas—1 comma *as* clause, 1 comma *if* clause, 1 comma introductory, 1 comma *when* clause; 1 semicolon because of comma; 2 missing words.

304.

(shorthand outlines) **(161)**

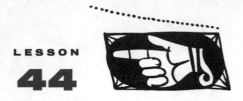

LESSON 44

▶ **Warmup.** Your warmup letter is No. 283 on page 234. Practice the sentence that makes up paragraph 3, breaking it into two or three parts.

305. Word Beginnings and Endings

Short-

Post-

Sub-

-gram

Short, shortly, shortage, shortest, shortcoming, shortsighted, shorthand, shortness.

Post office, postpone, postage, postal, postman, postmaster, postmark.

Submit, substantial, subscribed, subscriber, subscription, sublet, sublease, subway.

Program, telegram, radiogram, diagram, cablegram.

Reading and Writing Practice

306. Transcription Word Study

addressee   The one to whom a letter is addressed.

circulation   The number of copies of each issue of a magazine or a newspaper distributed to subscribers.

full-page ad   An advertisement that occupies an entire page in a newspaper or magazine.

307.

Transcribe:
$15
, as clause

addressee
whether
recommend

, introductory

; no conjunction
, introductory

(shorthand outlines)

(171)

308.

pleasure
, apposition
, as clause

circulation
, parenthetical

; no conjunction
, introductory

(138)

309.

*approaching
clients*

, introductory

full-page
   hyphenated
   before noun

area
, **conjunction**
, *when* **clause**

(151)

310.

Transcribe:
   April 16
, **apposition**

, *as* **clause**
Transcribe:
   $350

, **series**
; **because of comma**
, **introductory**

425/

(110)

311.

[shorthand outlines] **(138)**

▶ **Warmup.** As your final warmup for this chapter, make as many complete copies of letter No. 283 on page 234 as time permits. Write as rapidly as you can, but be sure that your notes are readable.

312. Vocabulary Builder

Men

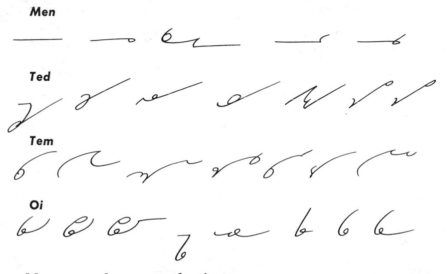

Ted

Tem

Oi

Men, many, salesmen, month, minute.
Invited, waited, treated, rated, deposited, study, steadily.
Item, temple, customer, estimate, attempt, system, tomorrow.
Point, appoint, appointment, enjoy, royal, join, boy, boil.

Reading and Writing Practice

313. Transcription Word Study

> **reception room** A room in which clients and visitors are received.

pressing Urgent

deadline The latest possible time by which something must be completed.

memoranda (plural of *memorandum*) Informal records, notes, or messages.

314.

[shorthand outlines]

, introductory
realize

[shorthand outlines]

yours
, conjunction

[shorthand outlines]

, introductory
questions

[shorthand outlines]

, series
, as clause
grateful

[shorthand outlines]

(140)

315.

; no conjunction
, introductory

[shorthand outlines]

, series
reception
appointment

, if clause
radio

45 ___   45 ___

. courteous
request

(158)

316.

customers
, parenthetical
; because of comma

well-organized
hyphenated
before noun

(76)

The businessman's most precious commodity is time. He has so much to do and so few hours in the day in which to do it that he is always ready to reward any employee who can save even a few minutes a day for him.

In the following story, you will see how Jim Green was able to save several hours for his employer each time he returned from a business trip.

317. Jim Green, Timesaver

[Shorthand text]

(302)

Check List

1. Why did Mr. Brown have to take several hours after he returned from a trip to determine what things needed immediate attention and what things could wait?

2. What did Jim do to save his employer's time?

3. What should you do when you work for your first employer?

CHAPTER Ten

Education

Education is probably the biggest "business" in our country today. Everyone is, at one time or another, one of its customers — and its customers are constantly increasing. In fact, they are increasing so rapidly that buildings cannot be put up fast enough to accommodate them.

Public schools in the United States employ thousands upon thousands of teachers, superintendents, and principals. Of course, these schools have need for vast numbers of office workers, too — bookkeepers, typists, filing clerks, telephone operators, and stenographers and secretaries. Similarly, colleges and universities, private business schools, trade schools, and other private schools employ hundreds of thousands of academic and office personnel. Most secretaries find their work in educational institutions interesting and exciting.

A stenographer in a high school principal's office put it this way: "My work never gets dull — every day is different — and there are so many young people to work with that I keep young, too!" A stenographer-receptionist in a private business school said she likes her job because "I greet all callers — businessmen, prospective students, and parents. I think the biggest thrill of my job is to see the change that takes place in a student — from the time he comes in to enroll until he graduates and takes an office position. They seem to 'grow' before my very eyes!"

Yes, the rewards of working in education are many. Perhaps you will have an opportunity to learn more about the advantages of this field by working during your free hours or after school in one of the school offices or, perhaps, as "secretary" to a faculty member. The letters in this chapter will give you some idea of the type of material that a stenographer in a school system takes from dictation.

318. Phrase Builder. There are 50 phrases in the following list. After you have read the phrases once forward, read them backward. Can you read them as rapidly backward as you can forward?

Will

With

You

Will be, will have, will not, will not be, will be able, will prove, will you.

With him, with those, with our, with reference, with such, with that, with the, with them, with these, with this, with us, with which, with which the, with you, with it.

You are, you are not, you can, you cannot, you could, you desire, you did not, you do not, you have, you have had, you have not, you know, you like, you made, you may, you may be, you may be sure, you may have, you might, you must, you need, you see, you should, you think, you will be, you will not, you would, you would be.

319.

[shorthand outlines]

(144)

Reading and Writing Practice

320. Transcription Word Study

grooming   Neatness, tidiness, smartness of appearance and dress.

occupation   A person's principal business or job. A person's principal source of livelihood.

remedial class   A class in which special help is given to students having difficulty with a subject.

321.

, apposition
Transcribe:
   October 1

necessarily
adjustments
, series

, introductory

, if clause
answer

(123)

322.

up-to-the-minute
   hyphenated
   before noun
, when clause

references
student's

, introductory
renewal

Transcribe:
$5
, conjunction

(142)

323.
, apposition
; because of comma
errors

children
admitted

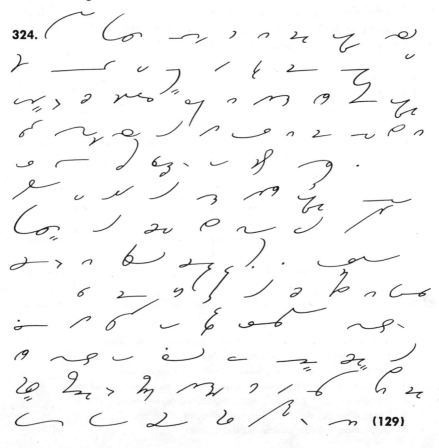

(104)

Transcription Quiz. For you to supply: 5 commas—1 comma parenthetical, 1 comma conjunction, 2 commas series, 1 comma *if* clause;
2 semicolons—1 semicolon no conjunction, 1 semicolon because of comma; 2 missing words.

324.

(129)

LESSON
47

▶ **Warmup.** Your warmup letter is No. 319 on page 260. Copy as much of the letter as time permits. Write as rapidly as you can, but be sure that your shorthand is readable.

325. Brief-Form Chart. The following chart contains 42 brief forms and derivatives. After you have read the complete chart from left to right, read down each column.

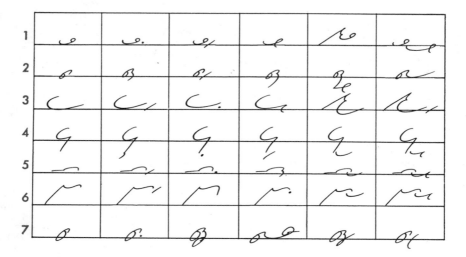

1. Regard, regarding, regarded, regards, disregard, regardless.
2. Use, uses, used, useful, usefulness, useless.
3. Please, pleased, pleasing, pleases, displease, displeased.
4. Purchase, purchases, purchasing, purchased, purchaser, purchasers.
5. Enclose, enclosed, enclosing, encloses, enclosure, enclosures.
6. Direct, directed, direction, directing, director, directors.
7. Out, outing, outside, outline, outset, output.

326. Geographical Expressions

[shorthand symbols]

Nashville, Danville, Knoxville, Jacksonville, Evansville, Brownsville, Zanesville, Louisville.

Indiana, Louisiana, Connecticut, Wisconsin, Florida, Georgia, Tennessee.

Reading and Writing Practice

327. Transcription Word Study

community A body of people living in the same place and under the same laws.

prominent Standing out, well known.

tuition The payment for instruction.

board Meals.

328. *[shorthand outlines]*

writer's
, parenthetical
; because of comma

, if clause
receive

[shorthand outlines]

, *as clause*
immediate

(114)

329.
, *apposition*
permission
referred

, *as clause*
husband

, *parenthetical*
, *introductory*

, *series*
community

, *parenthetical*
; *no conjunction*
, *introductory*

hesitate
connection
son's

(143)

330.

20

, when clause
individual
its

Transcribe:
$150
, introductory $\quad$ 9:30 $\quad$ 150/₇

(177)

331.

graduated
, as clause

accounting
tuition
, introductory

, as clause
part-time
  hyphenated
  before noun

(shorthand outline) **(102)**

Transcription Quiz. For you to supply: 8 commas—2 commas apposition, 1 comma conjunction, 2 commas parenthetical, 1 comma as clause, 2 commas if clause; 1 semicolon no conjunction; 2 missing words.

332.

(shorthand outline) **(153)**

▶ **Warmup.** Your warmup letter is No. 319 on page 260. This time, write as many copies of paragraph 1 as time permits. Strive to increase your speed with each writing.

333. Word Families

-logy

-mentary

-iate

-ctor

Psychology, biology, apology, geology, bacteriology.
Elementary, complimentary, supplementary, documentary.
Appreciate, associate, appropriate, substantiate, abbreviate, deviate, collegiate.
Instructor, contractor, conductor, collector, director.

Reading and Writing Practice

334. Transcription Word Study

elementary   Beginning.

associates Co-workers.

complimentary Expressing praise or congratulation.

335.

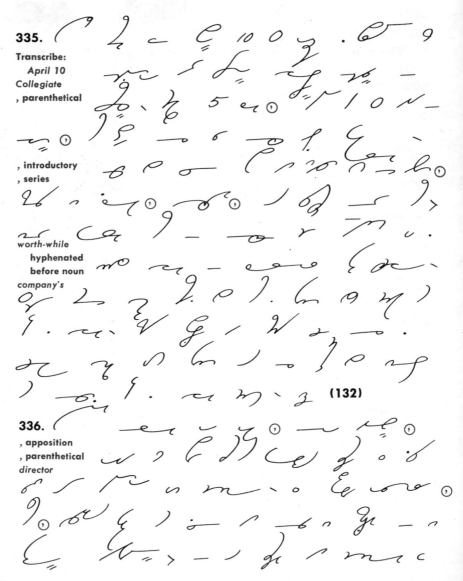

Transcribe:
April 10
Collegiate
, parenthetical

, introductory
, series

worth-while
hyphenated
before noun
company's

(132)

336.
, apposition
, parenthetical
director

, introductory

procedures
, introductory

schedules
, introductory

; because of comma
, when clause
appreciate

(164)

337.

, as clause
requested

, parenthetical
elementary

, apposition

18/

7"

25/

, conjunction

338.

, apposition
career

, series
, as clause
referring

(130)

(85)

339.

Transcribe:
$5
language

study
, series

investments
; no conjunction **(113)**

Transcription Quiz. For you to supply: 6 commas—2 commas series, 2 commas introductory, 1 comma conjunction, 1 comma *if* clause; 1 semicolon because of comma; 2 missing words.

340.

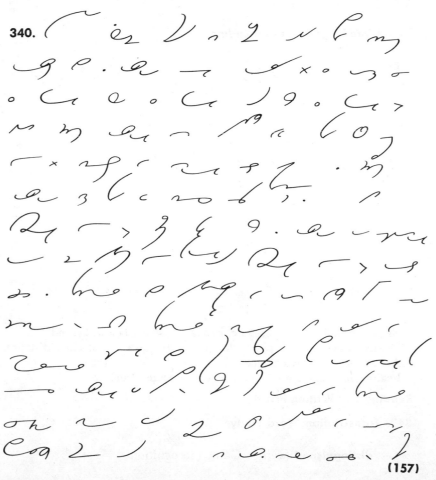

(157)

LESSON
49

▶ **Warmup.** Your warmup letter is No. 319 on page 260. Make as many copies of paragraphs 2 and 3 of the letter as you can. If you write a poor outline, don't stop to cross it out and rewrite it; just keep on writing.

341. Word Beginnings and Endings

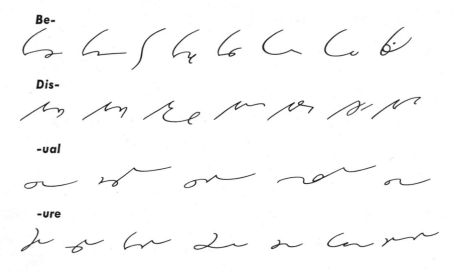

Be-

Dis-

-ual

-ure

Begin, become, before, because, beneath, belong, below, behind.
Discuss, discussion, displace, distract, distinguish, dissatisfied, distance.
Annual, schedule, actual, gradual, equal.
Feature, nature, picture, failure, secure, procure, structure.

Reading and Writing Practice

342. Transcription Word Study

distinguished (verb)   Gained recognition.

Parent-Teacher Association (often abbreviated to PTA)
An organization of parents and teachers, the purpose of
which is to establish a closer relationship between the
school and the family.

343.

, apposition
father-and-son
roast-beef
  hyphenated
  before noun

feature
distinguished

, if clause
enclosed

(129)

344.
Council
faculty
cordially

, apposition
, conjunction

275

, series
vice-president

; no conjunction
, introductory

(134)

345.

, as clause
student's
parents'

, if clause
actually
judgment

, apposition
; because of comma
, if clause

/ 10:30 ⓢ

(124)

346.

, parenthetical
son's

(140)

347.

approximately
children

, when clause
, parenthetical
co-operate

arrangement
, introductory
, series

(shorthand outlines) **(101)**

Transcription Quiz. For you to supply: 4 commas—1 comma when clause, 1 comma *if* clause, 2 commas introductory; 2 semicolons—1 semicolon because of comma, 1 semicolon no conjunction; 2 missing words.

348. *(shorthand outlines)* **(150)**

▶ **Warmup.** Your warmup letter for the final time is No. 319 on page 260. Write the last paragraph as rapidly as you can once. Then make one copy of the entire letter in your best shorthand.

349. Vocabulary Builder

Ld

Rd

Nt

Ow

Old, child, children, field, build, failed, nailed.
Board, insured, incurred, offered, neared, flattered, tired, scored.
Recent, applicant, superintendent, parent, won't, front, rent.
Doubt, now, power, shout, proud, loud, crowd, brow.

Reading and Writing Practice

350. Transcription Word Study

    sponsor (*verb*) Take responsibility for.

    prospective Confidently expected.

351.

sponsor
occasions

, if clause
convenient

(121)

352.

, introductory
; because of comma
vacancy

experience
superintendent
, series

, if clause
appreciate
Easter

, parenthetical
. courteous
request

(160)

353.

recommend
offered
, apposition

doctors'
nurses'
, series

worth-while
hyphenated
before noun

12

, when clause
formal

, if clause
attached

13 ^{50}

(154)

281

Secretarial Pointer

The good salesman seldom relies on an oral presentation alone to sell his product. He knows that one picture is worth a thousand words.

This is something you should remember when you try to sell your stenographic services to a prospective employer. Don't just tell him that you are a good shorthand writer; show him a certificate to prove it. Don't just tell him you know how to run a mimeograph; show him some samples of what you have done.

As you will see in the following story, Helen's evidence of her accomplishments in school paid big dividends!

354. Saved by a Scrapbook!

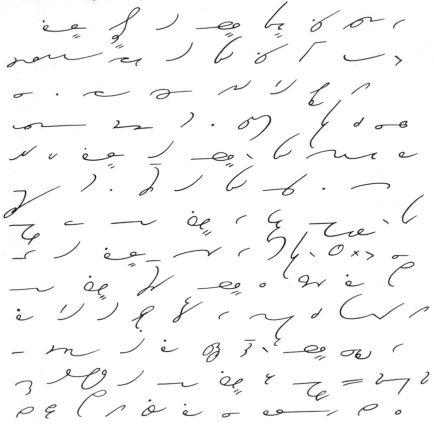

(288)

Check List

1. Why was Mr. Harris impressed with Mary?
2. Why did he hire Helen rather than Mary?
3. What do you plan to do as a result of Helen's experience?

Publishing

Did you ever think it might be fun to work in the office of a large magazine publisher? newspaper publisher? book publisher? If you have, you are no different from thousands of others! Many people are attracted to publishing work for various reasons.

Many young people who have a flair for writing have found that one of the best ways to get a job in a publishing office is through stenographic skills. Since it is not always easy to get an immediate position as a writer or a reporter, more and more young people have found careers in publishing through the "side door" — stenography. Many top-notch reporters and feature writers found their jobs in just this way.

If your ambitions to do editorial work should be realized, the work that lies ahead of you is varied and extremely interesting. In fact, it may truly be said that in itself editorial work is a continuing opportunity for obtaining a liberal education.

Whether you do editorial work or not, however, working in a publishing office is generally filled with activity and excitement. Here one has the feeling that he is in the very center of things. As a typist, as a stenographer, as a proofreader, or as a secretary, in publishing there is need for many different kinds of skills.

In this chapter you will have an opportunity to read and take from dictation material that pertains to publishing activities. Perhaps through these letters you can capture some of the flavor of this interesting work.

355. Phrase Builder. The following list contains 50 phrases that are frequently used in business letters. Can you read the entire list in 1 minute?

T for To

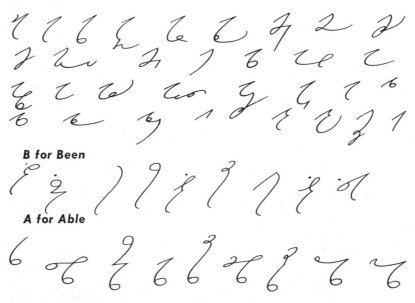

B for Been

A for Able

Is to be, to be, to be able, to be sure, to bring, to build, to change, to fill, to find, to fit, to follow, to finish, to have, to pay, to place, to please, to prepare, to present, to print, to protect, to provide, to brush, to put, to see, to say, to sell, to serve, to ship, to speak, to spend, to visit, to which.

Has been, has not been, have been, I have been, it has been, we have been, would have been, there has been, had been.

Be able, I may be able, I have not been able, to be able, we have been able, we may be able, we shall be able, he will be able, you will be able.

Warmup Phrase Letter. There are 34 phrases in the following 147-word warmup phrase letter. How fast can you read and copy the entire letter?

356.

(147)

Reading and Writing Practice

357. Transcription Word Study

walk of life   Station or place in life.

publications Books, magazines, newspapers, etc.

leisure time Time free from work; time available for pleasure and relaxation.

358.

, as clause
, apposition
; no conjunction

[shorthand outlines]

, introductory
businessmen

[shorthand outlines]

thereby ·
develop

[shorthand outlines]

, series
, if clause

[shorthand outlines] **(146)**

359.
country's
worth-while
hyphenated
before noun

[shorthand outlines] 204

campaigns
efficiently

. courteous
request

360. (110)

yours
, when clause

, introductory
; because of comma
human

, parenthetical
month's
believe

worth-while
hyphenated
before noun

[shorthand outline] , parenthetical
enclosed [shorthand outline] **(136)**

Transcription Quiz. For you to supply: 5 commas—1 comma apposition, 1 comma as clause, 1 comma conjunction, 2 commas series; 2 missing words.

361. [shorthand outlines]

[shorthand outlines] **(133)**

LESSON
52

▶ **Warmup.** Letter No. 356 on page 286. Practice as many of the sentences in paragraph 1 as time permits. Break down each sentence into several parts, and write each part three or four times as rapidly as you can.

362. Brief-Form Chart. There are 42 brief forms and derivatives in the following chart. After you have read the chart from left to right, read *down* each column. Can you read the brief forms down as rapidly as you can from left to right?

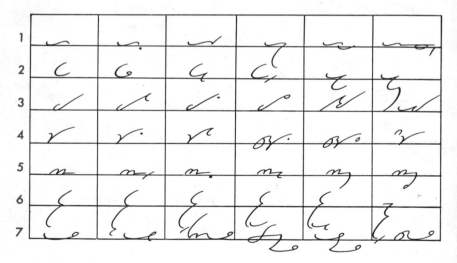

1. Work, working, worked, workable, worker, workmanship.
2. Present, presently, presents, presented, represent, representative.
3. Order, orders, ordering, orderly, disorder, reorder.
4. Stand, standing, stands, outstanding, outstandingly, understand.
5. Wonder, wondered, wondering, wonders, wonderful, wonderfully.
6. Publish, publishes, published, publisher, publishers, unpublished.
7. Let, lets, booklet, pamphlet, leaflet, outlet.

363. Geographical Expressions

[shorthand symbols]

Princeton, Evanston, Lewiston, Johnstown, Jamestown, Allentown.
Pennsylvania, Ohio, Virginia, West Virginia, Minnesota, Colorado,
Mississippi, Oregon.

Reading and Writing Practice

364. Transcription Word Study

lobby   A passage or hall that is large enough to be used
for a waiting room.

deductible   Able to be taken away or subtracted.

broad hint   An obvious indirect suggestion.

365. *[shorthand outlines]*

Worker's
, series

[shorthand outlines]

easy-to-read
hyphenated
before noun
, as clause

[shorthand outlines]

This page contains Gregg shorthand outlines with the following printed marginal notes and annotations:

, parenthetical
, series
Pennsylvania

366.

husband
, if clause

effect
Christmas

, if clause
; no conjunction

bowl
; no conjunction

, if clause
; because of comma
undoubtedly

(135)

367.

, when clause
Transcribe:
  18 Street

185

, conjunction
area

out-of-town
  hyphenated
  before noun

(124)

368.
, if clause
average
neglected

, parenthetical
medical
deductible

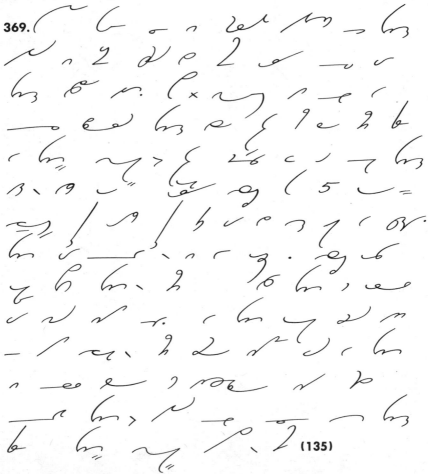

(110)

Transcription Quiz. For you to supply: 4 commas—1 comma *when* clause, 1 comma conjunction, 2 commas *if* clause; 2 semicolons no conjunction; 2 missing words.

369.

(135)

▶ **Warmup.** Letter No. 356 on page 286. Take the sentences in paragraph 2 for your warmup today. Break down each sentence into convenient parts.

370. Word Families

Some

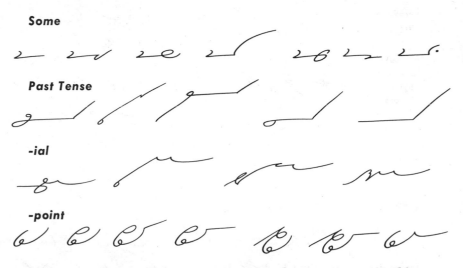

Past Tense

-ial

-point

Some, somewhat, somewhere, sometime, somehow, someone, something.
Examined, edited, determined, amounted, mounted.
Material, editorial, testimonial, industrial.
Point, appoint, appointed, appointment, disappoint, disappointment,
    pointless.

Reading and Writing Practice

371. Transcription Word Study

> **sales figures** A report of the number of copies of a book
>   that have been sold.

illustrated   Containing pictures, drawings, etc.

determined (*adjective*)   Firm, decided.

372.

, when clause
disappointed
history

, introductory
copies

, as clause
well-known
hyphenated
before noun

; because of comma
, introductory
testimonials

, parenthetical
success

, introductory
failure

(139)

373.

associate
pleasure
announce

, conjunction
Frank's

16

graduated
assistant

_ 1945 ... 15, 1946

9.

industrial
engineering

ab (158)

374.
, introductory
catalogue

, as clause
, parenthetical

major
, apposition

, series
author's

, introductory
description

, parenthetical
; because of comma
sincerely

40

. courteous
request

(157)

375.

; no conjunction

, introductory
, as clause

circulars
, series

20

30

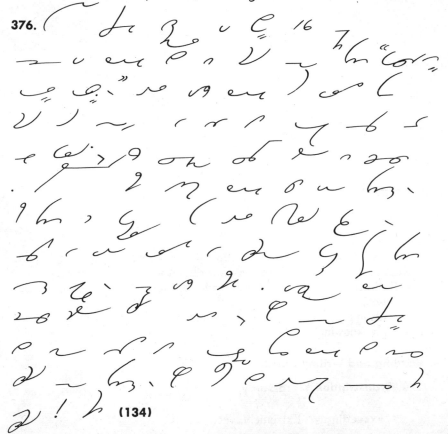

(144)

Transcription Quiz. For you to supply: 8 commas—1 comma apposition, 1 comma as clause, 2 commas introductory, 4 commas parenthetical; 1 semicolon no conjunction; 2 missing words.

376.

(134)

LESSON 54

▶ **Warmup.** Letter No. 356 on page 286. Take the sentences in the last paragraph. Remember, when you write an outline that is not entirely to your liking, don't stop but keep on writing.

377. Word Beginnings and Endings

Im-

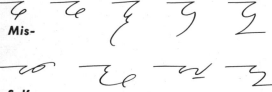

Mis-

Self-

-ingly

Impression, impress, impossible, improve, improvement, improper, import.
Mistake, misplace, misquote, misinform, misunderstand, mystery.
Self-addressed, self-educated, self-made, self-respect, self-interest, selfish, unselfish.
Astonishingly, surprisingly, willingly, accordingly, increasingly, exceedingly, knowingly.

Reading and Writing Practice

378. Transcription Word Study

exceedingly   Extremely, very.

table of contents A summary of the material in a book. It usually appears in the front of a book.

unselfish Thinking of others rather than of oneself.

379.

, as clause
, apposition
Principles

up to date
  no noun
  no hyphen

, conjunction

, conjunction
; because of comma
, series

(138)

380.

, series
wallets

impression
, parenthetical

enclosed
self-addressed

(128)

381.

well-known
  hyphenated
  before noun

chances
; no conjunction
, introductory

, parenthetical
, introductory

(144)

382.

(133)

Transcription Quiz. For you to supply: 5 commas—1 comma *if* clause, 1 comma *when* clause, 2 commas conjunction, 1 comma introductory; 2 semicolons because of comma; 2 missing words.

383.

(144)

► **Warmup.** Letter No. 356 on page 286. Write one complete copy of the letter. Write it in your best style of shorthand.

384. Vocabulary Builder

Omission of Ow

Omission of E in U

Omission of Short U

Omission of Minor Vowel

Brown, sound, found, announce, count, amount, discount.
New, produce, reduce, manuscript, volume, numerous.
Done, much, some, summer, rush, brush, clutch, judge.
Ideal, genuine, serious, various, tedious, courteous, theory, period.

Reading and Writing Practice

385. Transcription Word Study

> **manuscript** The author's typewritten copy of a book.
>
> **editing** Revising and preparing a manuscript for publication.

insatiable curiosity (*ĭn·sā'shĭ·à·b'l*) Curiosity that can
never be satisfied or fulfilled.

386. *[shorthand outlines]*

, conjunction
convinced

[shorthand outlines]

, as clause
; because of comma .
potential

[shorthand outlines]

, parenthetical
; because of comma

[shorthand outlines]

well-known
  hyphenated
  before noun

[shorthand outlines]

(131)

387. *[shorthand outlines]*

manuscript
, apposition
, conjunction

[shorthand outlines]

, parenthetical
electrical

[shorthand outlines]

(131)

388.

(110)

Some stenographers make the mistake of thinking that their days of study are over once they have left school. If they want to get ahead, however, they will quickly discover that their days of study have really just begun when they enter the business world.

The ambitious stenographer will try to learn all he can about the job ahead. Harry Brown, in the following story, never regretted that he had an insatiable curiosity about the job ahead.

389. Harry's Insatiable Curiosity

(327)

Check List

1. Why was Harry a dismay to his parents and teachers?
2. What did Harry's curosity lead him to do when he took his first position with a publishing firm?
3. How was Harry's curiosity rewarded when his superior was promoted?

Investments

Mr. Smith is an average American. His family is well provided for, he is buying his home, and he has put away some savings. In addition, he owns an adequate amount of insurance for the protection of his family. Mr. Smith has just received a sum of money that he does not need immediately for his daily living. He decides to invest it by buying a "share of business." He knows that, if he buys stock in a good strong company, he has an opportunity to earn money on his investment — in the form of dividends — in addition to having a relatively safe place for his investment. Of course, if he buys stock in a business about which he knows very little, expecting to make a large amount of money on his investments, he stands a risk of losing everything.

How can Mr. Smith tell which company is safe and is most likely to give him a fair return on his investment? If he is wise, he will consult a broker or an investment counselor. It is the business of such counselors to know about all types of investments.

Millions of Americans like Mr. Smith invest money every day in business. Such investments are a necessary part of our system of business. Without the money of investors, many large businesses simply could not bring to us the products and services we enjoy. For example, your telephone company, the company that manufactures the automobile your family drives, the company that publishes your favorite magazine — all depend on the investor's money for carrying on their business and expanding it for better production. Thus, the investment counselor is an important person in American business.

Investment counselors are usually situated in larger cities and are generally near the financial district — such as LaSalle Street in Chicago, Montgomery Street in San Francisco, Wall Street in New York, etc. There are investment counselors in most medium- and large-sized cities.

If you were to work in the office of an investment counselor, you might take from dictation letters similar to those in this chapter.

390. Phrase Builder. The phrases in this lesson are frequently used in everyday correspondence. A number of them appear in your warmup letter and in the other letters in the chapter.

Is Not, Was Not

Want

Ago

It is not, it isn't, he was not, I was not, was not, it wasn't, if it is not, if it wasn't.

I want, he wants, he wanted, if you want, we want, we wanted, you want, they want.

Few days ago, few months ago, long ago, months ago, several months ago, some time ago, weeks ago, years ago.

▶ **Warmup Phrase Letter.** The following 120-word letter contains 31 frequently used business phrases. Can you read the letter in 60 seconds or less? After you have read the letter, can you copy it in 2 minutes?

391.

(shorthand outline)

(120)

Reading and Writing Practice

392. Transcription Word Study

dividends   The share in the profits of a corporation that stockholders receive.

securities   Stocks and bonds.

stable   Firmly established, fixed.

investment counselor   One who advises investors on what stocks to buy and when to sell.

393.

, parenthetical
steady

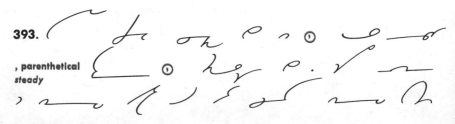

; because of comma
, as clause
choose

securities
regardless

, if clause
Transcribe:
$1

advantage
; no conjunction

(164)

394.

, introductory
Government
, apposition

conjunction
acceptance

response
previous

313

(119)

395.

minute's
, introductory

believe
tapping

, introductory
counselors

, when clause
assist

(153)

396.

[shorthand outlines]

(167)

▶ **Warmup.** Letter No. 391 on page 311. Write as rapidly as possible as much of the letter as time permits.

397. Brief-Form Chart. The following chart contains 42 brief forms and derivatives.

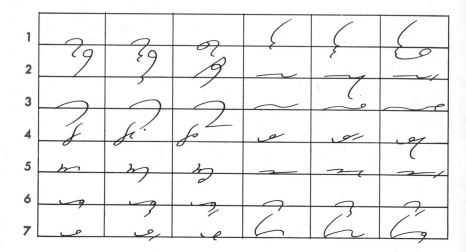

1. Company-keep, companies-keeps, accompany; business, businesses, business-like.
2. Advantage, advantages, disadvantage; Mr.-market, marketable, marketed.
3. Govern, governing, government; glad, gladly, gladness.
4. Particular, particulars, particularly; return, returned, returnable.
5. Success, successful, successfully; number, numbers, numbered.
6. Request, requests, requested; question, questions, questioned.
7. Regard, regarded, regards; big, bigger, biggest.

398. Geographical Expressions

[shorthand outlines]

Washington, Bloomington, Burlington, Lexington, Huntington.
Maryland, Michigan, Missouri, Texas, Wisconsin, Wyoming, Nevada,
Vermont.

Reading and Writing Practice

399. Transcription Word Study

"tip on the market"   Hint, based on secret information,
as to which stocks are going to go up.

forged ahead   Moved ahead steadily.

400. *[shorthand outlines]*

, conjunction
whether

, series
emergencies
already

, parenthetical
lying

[shorthand outlines]

(140)

401.

*successful
company's*

*future
, if clause*

*employees
companies*

, if clause

(151)

402.

*mysterious
, introductory*

, when clause

American

despite

economic

, introductory

realize

, as clause

investors

; because of comma

, parenthetical

purchase

, apposition

(167)

403.

investing

, if clause

, apposition

easy-to-understand
hyphenated
before noun

, if clause
, series
surprising

(114)

Transcription Quiz. For you to supply: 7 commas—1 comma as clause, 1 comma apposition, 1 comma conjunction, 2 commas introductory, 2 commas parenthetical; 2 missing words.

404.

16

1930

1930   1940

1945   14,

(167)

▶ **Warmup.** Letter No. 391 on page 311. Break up the sentences in paragraph 1 into convenient groups, and write each group several times as rapidly as possible.

405. Word Families

-tal

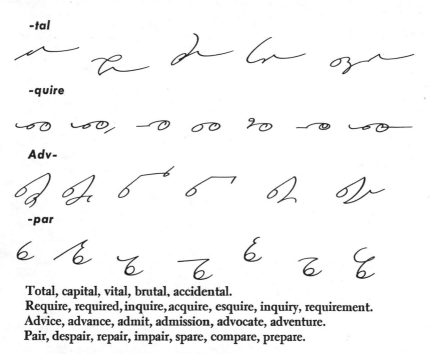

-quire

Adv-

-par

Total, capital, vital, brutal, accidental.
Require, required, inquire, acquire, esquire, inquiry, requirement.
Advice, advance, admit, admission, advocate, adventure.
Pair, despair, repair, impair, spare, compare, prepare.

Reading and Writing Practice

406. Transcription Word Study

> **similarly** In much the same way.

advocate To recommend or approve a particular thing or idea.

impair To lessen the quality, value, or strength of a thing.

restricting Holding back or limiting.

407.

, as clause
success

similarly
, introductory

spare
, conjunction

inquiry
, series

(110)

408.

569

, parenthetical
, introductory
varies

; no conjunction
, introductory
average

, if clause
postal

569

, if clause
; no conjunction
advise

worth-while

hyphenated
before noun

(129)

409.

, parenthetical
; because of comma
expense

advocate
acquire

, apposition
adequate

[Shorthand outlines]

, when clause
discuss

(164)

410.
ancient
patient
occasional

, introductory
; no conjunction
, introductory

impaired
organization's
primary

. courteous
request
peace

(110)

411.

capital
growth
, introductory

[shorthand outline]

, parenthetical
amount

. courteous
request

(90)

Transcription Quiz. For you to supply: 6 commas—2 commas apposition, 1 comma *when* clause, 2 commas parenthetical, 1 comma *if* clause; 1 semicolon no conjunction; 2 missing words.

412. *[shorthand outline]*

(135)

LESSON
59

▶ **Warmup.** Letter No. 391 on page 311. Break up the sentences in paragraph 2 into convenient groups, and write each group several times as rapidly as possible.

413. Word Beginnings and Endings

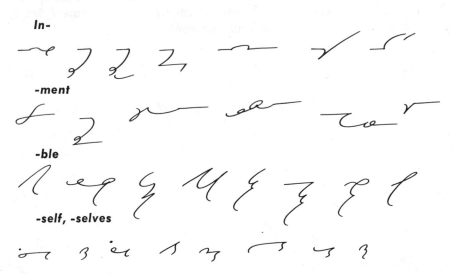

In-

-ment

-ble

-self, -selves

Increase, invest, investor, information, income, instead, intended.
Payment, investment, settlement, retirement, employment, statement.
Double, reliable, profitable, dependable, possible, impossible, capable, table.
Himself, yourself, herself, itself, oneself, themselves, ourselves, yourselves.

Reading and Writing Practice

414. Transcription Word Study

terminate To end.

reinvestment Buying securities with money earned from investments.

joint ownership Property owned by two or more persons.

dispense (*verb*) To distribute, to administer.

415.
, *as clause*
; *because of comma*
reinvestment

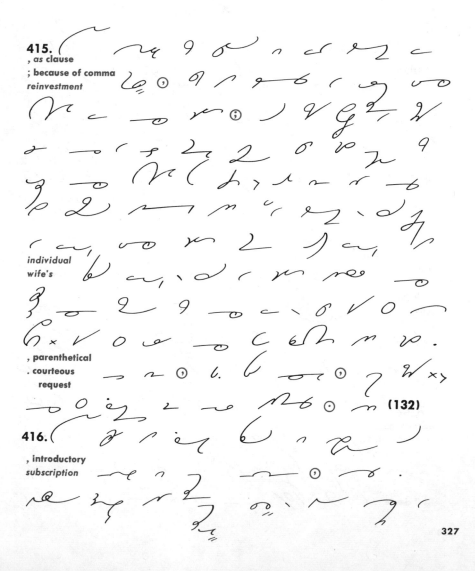

individual
wife's

, *parenthetical*
. *courteous*
   request

(132)

416.
, *introductory*
subscription

financial
today's

, when clause
handle
foresight

417.

(122)

, conjunction

income-producing
get-rich-quick
    hyphenated
    before noun
; no conjunction

long-range
    hyphenated
    before noun

, if clause

Proportion Check List

Do you find that you occasionally have difficulty reading the shorthand that you write? If you do, the cause may lie with your proportions. You will find your shorthand easier to read if you make

1. The large circles *huge*; the small circles *tiny*.

2. The short straight strokes, like *n* and *t*, very short; the long straight strokes, like *men* and *ted*, very long.

Also, be sure to make the curved strokes deep.

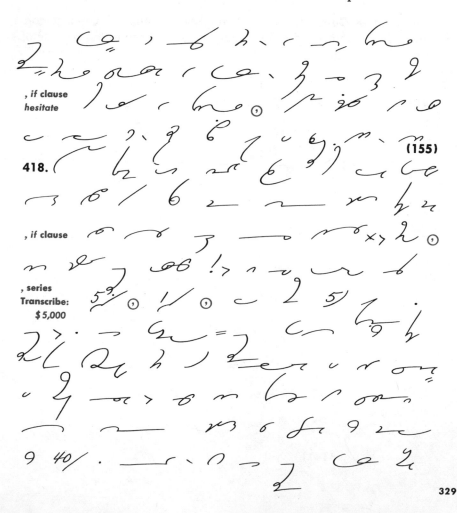

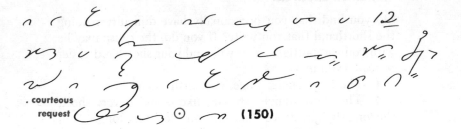

(150)

Transcription Quiz. For you to supply—6 commas—2 commas conjunction, 2 commas series, 2 commas *if* clause; 1 semicolon because of comma; 2 missing words.

419.

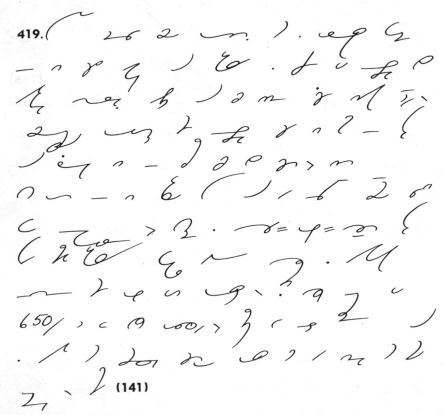

(141)

▶ **Warmup.** Letter No. 391 on page 311. In your best shorthand make a copy of the entire letter.

420. Vocabulary Builder

Fine, find, excite, provide, sacrifice, pride, might, item.
Own, owner, known, stop, stock, job, call, small.
Who, do, us, discuss, move, lose, trust, group.
Now, cow, proud, crowd, doubt, doubtless, undoubtedly.

Reading and Writing Practice

421. Transcription Word Study

> **in trust**   Held by one person for the benefit of another.
>
> **dependent**   One who relies on another for support.

422.

, when clause

customers
, as clause

, introductory
group

well-trained
    hyphenated
    before noun

; no conjunction
, introductory
, conjunction

, apposition
; because of comma
answer

(154)

423.

332

, parenthetical
lost

, introductory
difficulty

(127)

424.

, parenthetical
comprising

450,

, introductory
annual

(109)

Secretarial Pointer

One thing that a businessman finds hard to forgive and forget is a violation of his confidence. The businessman wants to feel that anything that is said or anything that happens in his office will never be discussed outside his office.

A person who discusses his employer's affairs outside the office is not welcome, no matter how good a worker he may be.

In the following story, Eleanor violates her employer's confidence unintentionally, which is equally unforgivable.

425. Strictly Confidential

[Shorthand notation] (312)

Check List

1. Why was Eleanor enthusiastic about her job?
2. How did she violate her employer's confidence?
3. How can Eleanor be sure she does not give away office secrets, even unintentionally?

PART THREE

Taking Dictation in a Business Office

COULD YOU TAKE a letter from a businessman if you were called upon to do so? If you have been reading and copying each day's lesson each day, you probably could, provided the letter was not too difficult or was not dictated too fast.

You would, however, find the dictation of a businessman a little different from the dictation that you have probably been taking in class. In class, your teacher's main task has been to develop your shorthand speed as rapidly as possible. Your teacher knows that the best way to do this is to have you practice under the most favorable conditions. That is why his dictation has been smooth and even, with every word spoken clearly and distinctly.

Your teacher knows that, when you are striving to increase your speed, your attention should be completely occupied with writing and should not be distracted by problems of hearing. Furthermore, your teacher has probably timed most of your dictation, as that is the only way your skill development can be determined.

The businessman, however, is not concerned with developing your speed; he assumes that you have the necessary skill to take down what he says. His dictation will not always be smooth; in fact, it may on occasion be choppy — sometimes fast, sometimes slow. Occasionally, his mind will be so occupied with the thought he is trying to express that he may slur some of his words. What is more, he may sometimes change his mind about a word or phrase and substitute another that he thinks expresses more clearly what he wants to say. He may delete, insert, or even transpose words.

You will quickly become accustomed to this type of office-style dictation if you have sufficient shorthand speed. The more speed you possess, the easier office-style dictation will be for you. Therefore, strive to build your shorthand speed to the highest point possible; you will always be glad that you did!

In the following lessons you will become familiar with some of the problems you will meet when you take office-style dictation. You will be given suggestions on how to handle each problem and shown how to handle it in your shorthand notes.

INSTRUCTIONS DURING DICTATION

A businessman will not only make deletions, insertions, and transpositions during dictation, but he also may ask you, right in the middle of a sentence, to check a date or an amount or the spelling of a name.

When he does this, the easiest way to indicate his instructions in your notes is to write in shorthand the word *check* in parentheses, close to the item to be checked. The businessman may say:

> We had a call from your representative, Mr. May, or was his name Gray? Please check that.

This will appear in your notes as follows:

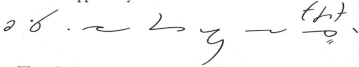

Then, before you transcribe, you will go to previous correspondence, the files, or any other source from which you can obtain the necessary information and "check."

CHAPTER THIRTEEN

Real Estate

When Frank and Mary Brown were married, they lived in an apartment. Like most married couples, however, they looked forward to the day when they would own their own home in which they could bring up their children and take part in community life. They did more than look forward to it; they planned for it and saved for it. By the time they were ready to buy a home, they knew in which town they wanted to live, how big a house they wanted, and how much they could afford to pay for it.

They then went to a reputable real estate agent in that town and told him their needs. The real estate agent—whose business it is to know which houses are for sale, how many rooms they have, in what condition they are, and what their prices are—was able to show Frank and Mary several houses in which he thought they would be interested. Finally, he showed them just the house they wanted.

The real estate agent then received from the seller a commission of 5 per cent of the selling price.

When Frank and Mary wish to sell their house for some reason, they will simply tell the real estate agent the price that they will accept for it, and he will procure a buyer for them, just as he had procured Frank and Mary for the seller from whom they bought the house.

The real estate agent is an important cog in every community. If you should be employed as a stenographer in a real estate office, you will probably take from dictation letters similar to the ones in this chapter.

426. Phrase Builder. The following list contains 30 phrases. These phrases illustrate the omission of an unimportant word in a phrase. How fast can you read the entire list?

A Omitted

And Omitted

Of Omitted

Or Omitted

As a result, at a loss, at a time, for a long time, in a position, for a moment. More and more, men and women, here and there, up and down, now and then.

Line of business, many of them, one of our, one of the, one of them, one of these, one of those, out of the, out of town, some of our, some of the, some of them, some of these.

More or less, day or two, one or two, two or three, once or twice, week or two ago.

▶ **Warmup Phrase Letter.** The following 177-word letter contains 38 phrases. This is your warmup letter for this chapter. How fast can you read and copy it?

427. *[Shorthand outlines]* **(177)**

Reading and Writing Practice

428. Transcription Word Study

Realty Board An association of real estate brokers.

list a house To place a house or other property in the hands of a real estate agent for sale or rental.

comparable Alike, or almost alike; similar.

429.

Transcribe:
32 Street
properties

[shorthand]

prospect
, apposition
; because of comma

[shorthand]

Transcribe:
$18,000
, as clause

[shorthand]

, conjunction
worth-while
hyphenated
before noun

[shorthand]

, introductory
, parenthetical
amount

[shorthand]

(148)

430.

[shorthand]

, as clause
probably
previous

[shorthand]

, *if clause*
. *courteous*
   request

(shorthand outlines)

; *because of comma*
, *if clause*
convenience

(139)

431.

, *when clause*
Realty

(shorthand outlines) **20**

maximum
possible

enclosed
; *no conjunction*

already
, *if clause*

up to date
   no noun,
   no hyphen

(132)

432.

[shorthand outlines]

(158)

OFFICE-STYLE DICTATION, 1

It is a very simple matter, in office-style dictation, to indicate in your notes that the dictator wishes to take out a word or a phrase. He may say:

> He bought a large but comfortable house in Spring-
> field—no, take out *comfortable*.

Sometimes he may go back and repeat the sentence without the word or the phrase that he wishes to omit. He may say:

> He bought a large but comfortable house in Spring-
> field—no, *he bought a large house in Springfield*.

To indicate this deletion, you would mark out in your notes not only the word *comfortable* but the word *but* as well.

If only a word or two is to be taken out, use a single, long, heavy backward stroke; if several words are to be taken out, a wavy line is preferable.

433. Illustration of Office-Style Dictation

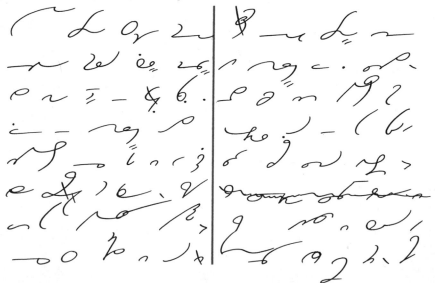

▶ **Warmup.** Your warmup letter is No. 427 on page 340. Write the first paragraph as rapidly as you can and as many times as you can in the time you have available.

434. Brief-Form Chart. The following chart contains 42 brief forms and derivatives. Can you read the entire chart in a minute or less?

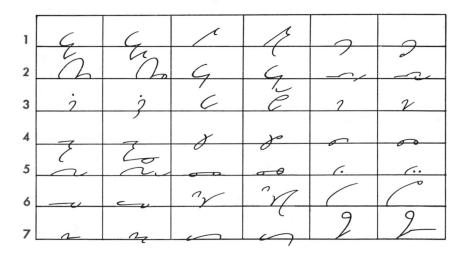

1. Property, properties, Dear Sir-desire, desirable, confidence-confident, confidently.
2. Difficult, difficulty, purchase, purchaser, enclosed, enclosure.
3. House, houses, part, apart, usual-wish, wished.
4. Newspaper, newspaperman, satisfy-satisfactory, satisfactorily, weak-week, weekly.
5. Great, greater, immediate, immediately, thing-think, thinking.
6. Most, almost, understand, understandable, time, timely.
7. One-won, once, organize, organization, advertise, advertisement.

435. Geographical Expressions

Hartford, Stamford, Bradford, Oxford, Radford, Bedford.
Connecticut, Rhode Island, Mississippi, North Dakota, South Dakota,
South Carolina, North Carolina.

Reading and Writing Practice

436. Transcription Word Study

asking price The figure at which the owner says he will
sell his house.

exterior Outer, outside.

breaking ground Preparing the site on which a house
is to be built.

durable Strong; capable of lasting a long time.

437.

, introductory
, conjunction
entertain

Transcribe:
  12 Street
, as clause

, series

, when clause

next-door

   hyphenated

   before noun

, apposition   **(127)**

438.

enough

whether

, if clause

endeavor

; because of (comma

, if clause

   (146)

439.

families

, introductory

steel
, series

; no conjunction
, series
stairs

fireproof
, as clause
; no conjunction

Transcribe:

$10,000

. courteous
request
convenient

(156)

440.

country
, if clause

well-built
hyphenated
before noun

. courteous
request

, if clause
appointment

(100)

Transcription Quiz. For you to supply: 5 commas—1 comma introductory, 2 commas parenthetical, 1 comma *if* clause, 1 comma apposition; 1 semicolon no conjunction; 2 missing words.

441.

(157)

LESSON
63

▶ **Warmup.** Your warmup letter is No. 427 on page 340. Copy the second paragraph as rapidly as you can and as many times as you can in the few minutes that you have available.

442. Word Families

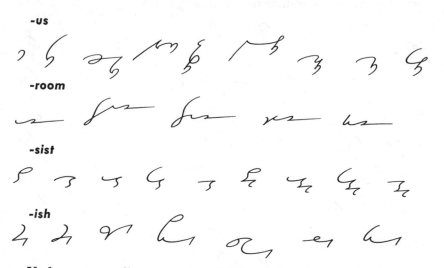

-us

-room

-sist

-ish

Us, bus, campus, discuss, spacious, delicious, cautious, conscious, precious.
Room, bedroom, bathroom, storeroom, showroom.
Assist, consist, resist, persist, insist, assistance, resistance, persistence, insistence.
Furnish, finish, astonish, abolish, accomplish, nourish, polish.

Reading and Writing Practice

443. Transcription Word Study

> **furnished apartment**   An apartment in which the furniture and, sometimes, dishes, linens, etc., are provided.

picture window An extra-large window, usually in a living room, facing an attractive view.

444.

master's
; no conjunction
, introductory

, series
, introductory
campus

, apposition

(140)

445.

, if clause
commuters

, when clause
blocks

efficiently
, conjunction

, series
four-room
hyphenated
before noun

, conjunction

150

(120)

446.

, parenthetical
apartments

, when clause
thousands
streaming

(65)

447.

, parenthetical
appreciate

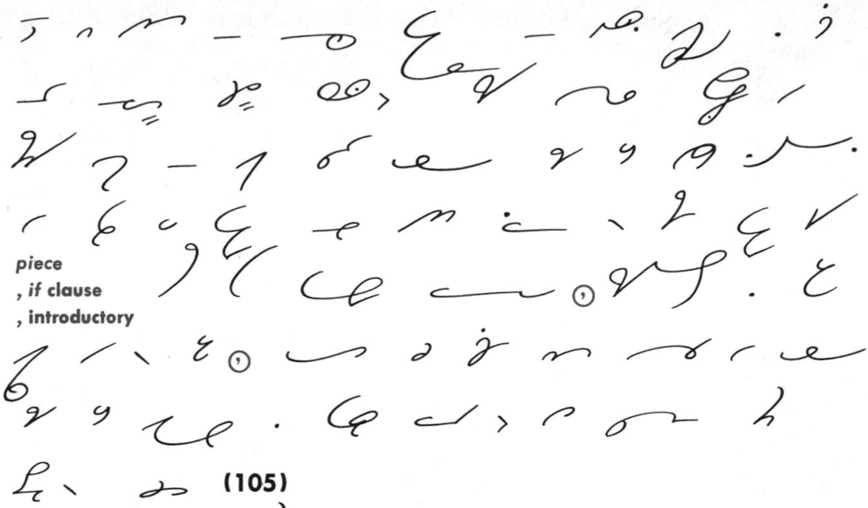

piece
, if clause
, introductory

(105)

448.

selection
available

, introductory
hundreds
columns

(114)

353

Transcription Quiz. For you to supply: 4 commas—2 commas *as* clause, 1 comma introductory, 1 comma *if* clause; 2 semicolons no conjunction; 2 missing words.

449.

[shorthand outlines]

(138)

▶ **Warmup.** Write paragraph 3 of letter No. 427 on page 340 as rapidly and as often as time permits.

450. Word Beginnings and Endings

-lity

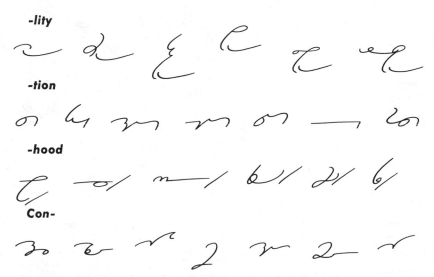

-tion

-hood

Con-

Quality, facility, possibility, ability, inability, reliability.
Action, portion, construction, instruction, attraction, mention, fraction.
Neighborhood, manhood, womanhood, childhood, fatherhood, boyhood.
Consequently, concern, contains, convenient, construct, confirm, contain.

Reading and Writing Practice

451. Transcription Word Study

> **completion**   Conclusion; the bringing to an end.
>
> **excavating**   Digging out and removing, as earth.

muffled Deadened or dulled.

subdivide Break up into two or more parts.

452.

, conjunction
, introductory
choice

completion
, conjunction

, introductory

, introductory
; no conjunction

, introductory
neighborhood

consequently
, introductory
, apposition

, conjunction
alternative

(173)

453.

, as clause
21-story
  hyphenated .
  before noun

[shorthand]

; because of comma
, parenthetical

[shorthand]

schedule
weeks'
excavating

[shorthand]

, as clause
outdoor
muffled

[shorthand]

neighborhood

(134)

454.

, parenthetical
occupies
lease

[shorthand]

subdivide
, parenthetical

[shorthand]

357

require
, if clause

(119)

455.

expire
, when clause

entrances
, conjunction

available

(140)

456.

; no conjunction

358

(84)

Transcription Quiz. For you to supply: 4 commas—1 comma as clause, 1 comma conjunction, 2 commas parenthetical; 2 semicolons—1 semicolon because of comma, 1 semicolon no conjunction; 2 missing words.

457.

(137)

LESSON 65

▶ **Warmup.** For the final time, your warmup letter will be No. 427 on page 340. In your best shorthand, copy as much of the letter as time permits.

458. Vocabulary Builder

Omission of T

Omission of D

Ng

Amounts

Fact, exact, contact, invest, interest, latest, smartest, neatest.
Extend, intend, pretend, mind, remind, demand, diamond.
Bring, spring, ring, sing, king, bungalow, single, strong.
$2; $1,000; $10,000; $100,000; 3,000,000; $300,000,000; 7,000,000,000.

Reading and Writing Practice

459. Transcription Word Study

    outskirts Edges or borders.

bungalow A one-story dwelling, often found at vacation
resorts.

460.

, introductory
bear
choose

Guide
, apposition

Transcribe:
$2
, introductory

(137)

461.

company's
, apposition
, as clause

, when **clause**
requirements
notified

(122)

462.

exactly
, parenthetical

, parenthetical
Transcribe:
  $18,000

well kept
  no noun,
  no hyphen

, if clause

(142)

463.

, apposition
bungalow

[shorthand outlines]

, conjunction

[shorthand outlines]

; no conjunction 12 [shorthand outlines] 18 [shorthand outlines]

[shorthand outlines]

, if clause

[shorthand outlines]

, parenthetical
; because of comma
available

[shorthand outlines]

(113)

464.

pleasure
, apposition

[shorthand outlines]

, parenthetical
obligation

[shorthand outlines]

(67)

363

How rapidly should a stenographer be able to write shorthand? The faster the better! True, when times are good and businessmen need all the office help they can get, they may hire stenographers who have little shorthand speed; but as soon as business falls off, those stenographers are the first to be let out.

Harriet, in the following story, would probably be the very first one to go!

465. The Importance of Shorthand Speed

[shorthand outlines]

[Shorthand symbols] (307)

Check List

1. Why was Harriet tired at the end of each day?

2. Why was Mary, on the other hand, as fresh as a daisy?

3. How high should you develop your shorthand speed?

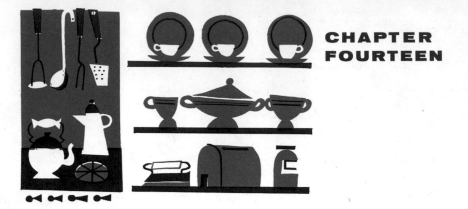

Home and Home Furnishings

Millions of Americans own their own homes. Millions of others are dreaming of the day when they can find a quiet spot in a rural setting where they can raise their children, do a bit of gardening, and "putter" around with a paint brush in one hand and a trowel in the other. Whereas some years ago a typical homeowner wouldn't have dared try to paint his house, decorate the interior, or lay a tile floor, today's "man of the house" (and woman, too!) pictures himself as a very handy person who isn't afraid to tackle anything. A great many husband-and-wife teams have built their own houses.

Because so many Americans are investing their spare time in improving their homes, the do-it-yourself business is booming. Magazines that cater to the home decorator or the handyman are more popular than ever. Paint stores, hardware stores, lumberyards, and decorator shops have geared their operations to this onslaught of new customers. Many stores have set up demonstration workshops, so that the customer may see for himself how a chair is upholstered or a room is painted. Booklets can be obtained on how to build a summer cabin, how to do vegetable gardening for fun and profit, and even on how to construct a swimming pool in the backyard!

The letters in this chapter concern the business of selling and servicing the homeowner. Perhaps through these letters you will get a better insight into the exciting activities — and problems — of America's new "class" — the landowner.

466. Phrase Builder. The following list contains 19 frequently used phrases. Can you read the entire list in less than half a minute?

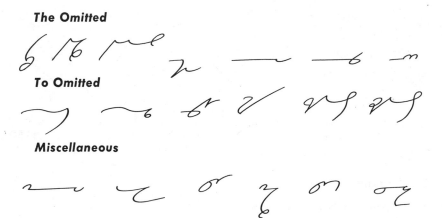

The Omitted

To Omitted

Miscellaneous

By the way, during the past, during the last, in the future, in the market, in the matter, in the world.

Glad to have, glad to see, in addition to the, up to date, I should like to have, we should like to have.

One of the most, will you please, out of the, one of the best, out of the question, I am of the opinion.

▶ **Warmup Phrase Letter.** The following 150-word letter contains 31 phrases. Read and copy this letter as rapidly as you can.

467.

[Shorthand outlines]

(150)

Reading and Writing Practice

468. Transcription Word Study

hollow *(adjective)* Empty; not solid or filled out.

fuel economy Using the minimum of gas or oil to get the maximum of heat.

469. *[Shorthand outlines]*

, as clause
, apposition
64-page
  hyphenated
  before noun

— 1920
, as clause
especially
, series

[Shorthand page — Gregg shorthand outlines]

, if clause
, apposition

216

territory
, conjunction

(150)

470.

b.

Wilson's
, parenthetical

installation
; no conjunction
, introductory

30,

, if clause
advantage

(146)

471.

, when clause
expense

appearance
applied

, when clause
consult

(108)

472.

, introductory
estimate

475

sandpaper
woodwork

(74)

Transcription Quiz. For you to supply: 4 commas—1 comma *as* clause, 1 comma apposition, 1 comma introductory, 1 comma *when* clause; 1 semicolon no conjunction; 2 missing words.

473.

(shorthand outlines)

(140)

OFFICE-STYLE DICTATION, 2

Occasionally, a businessman will dictate a word or a phrase and then change his mind and substitute another word or phrase. He may say:

> I want to purchase a cheap — no, *inexpensive* air-conditioning unit.

When that happens, the writer would simply place a line through the word *cheap* and write *inexpensive* right next to it.

Sometimes the dictator may change his mind about a word or a phrase after he has completed a sentence. He may say:

> I want to purchase a cheap air-conditioning unit — change that to *inexpensive*.

In this case, the writer would place a line through the word *cheap* and would write *inexpensive* above it.

If several words are to be deleted, it is usually better to use a wavy line to indicate the deletion.

474. Illustration of Office-Style Dictation

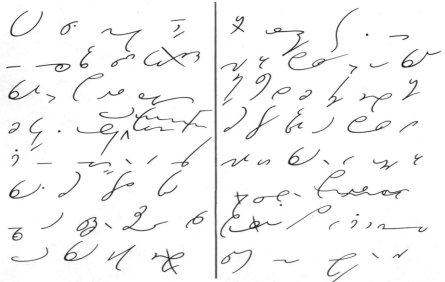

▶ **Warmup.** Your warmup letter is No. 467 on page 367. Write the first paragraph of that letter as rapidly as you can and as often as time permits.

475. Brief-Form Chart. There are 42 brief forms and derivatives in the following chart. Can you read the entire chart in a half a minute or less?

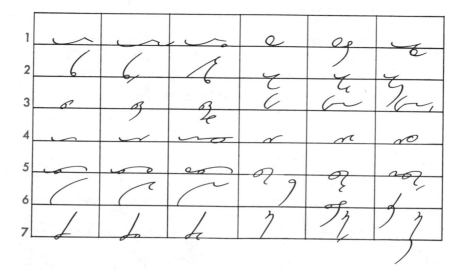

1. Long, longer, longingly; where, wherever, elsewhere.
2. Believe, believed, disbelieve; represent, represents, representative.
3. Use, useful, usefulness; part, partner, partnership.
4. Work, worked, workman; other, others, otherwise.
5. Regular, regularly, irregular; accompany, accompanies, unaccompanied.
6. Time, times, timer; ever, whenever, whichever.
7. General, generally, generals; suggest, suggested, suggestive.

476. Geographical Expressions

[shorthand outlines]

Davenport, Bridgeport, Westport, Logansport, Newport, Shreveport, Gulfport.

Louisiana, Iowa, Montana, Nebraska, New Mexico, Wyoming, Utah.

Reading and Writing Practice

477. Transcription Word Study

air conditioner An appliance that supplies the right amount of moisture and keeps the air in a room or a house cool in warm weather and warm in cold weather.

chore A small or odd job that has to be done.

478.

[shorthand outlines]

, parenthetical
unusually

air conditioner
, conjunction

, apposition

374

(145)

479.

, series
; no conjunction
coming

night's

, conjunction
sill

, if clause
16-page
hyphenated
before noun
; no conjunction

16 =

(135)

480.

, introductory
Monday's
chore

switch
, series

its
superiority
minutes'

, introductory
Transcribe:
  $300

(119)

481.

howl

, when clause
automatically

376

, series
, conjunction
convince

, as clause
obligation

(105)

Transcription Quiz. For you to supply: 4 commas—2 commas apposition, 2 commas *if* clause; 1 semicolon no conjunction; 1 missing word.

482.

(113)

LESSON 68

▶ **Warmup.** Your warmup phrase letter is No. 467 on page 367. Copy the second paragraph of this letter as rapidly as you can and as often as time permits.

483. Word Families

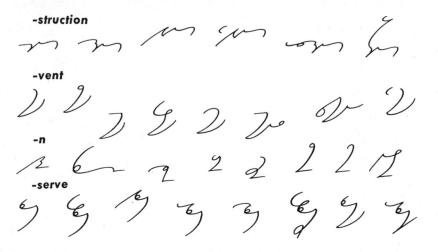

-struction

-vent

-n

-serve

Instruction, construction, destruction, self-destruction, reconstruction, obstruction.
Vent, event, invent, prevent, convent, inventory, adventure, circumvent.
Dozen, bargain, kitchen, often, fasten, even, oven, driven.
Serve, preserve, deserve, reserve, conserve, preservation, servant, reserved.

Reading and Writing Practice

484. Transcription Word Study

amateur   One who follows an occupation for pleasure rather than for business.

inventory The amount and value of goods or stock on hand.

suite (pronounced *swēt*) A set of matched furniture for a specific room.

485.
kitchen
storage
efficient

[shorthand outlines]

Transcribe:
$180
, apposition
, parenthetical

[shorthand outlines]

amateur
, conjunction

[shorthand outlines]

six-inch
hyphenated
before noun
, conjunction
. courteous
request

[shorthand outlines]

(139)

486.

[shorthand outlines]

; no conjunction

necessarily
character
, introductory

builder's
, introductory

(90)

487.
, series
clothing
furniture

destruction
enlightening

, if clause
. courteous
request

; no conjunction *[shorthand outline]*

(109)

488. *[shorthand outline]*

50

, introductory
maximum *[shorthand outline]*

, when clause
surprisingly *[shorthand outline]*

(114)

489. *[shorthand outline]*

beautiful
, apposition *[shorthand outline]*

Smith's
preserves *[shorthand outline]*

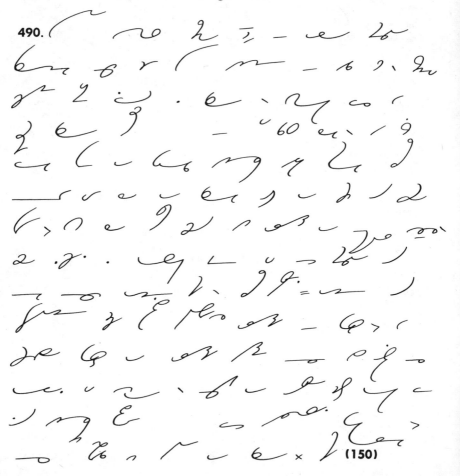

(89)

Transcription Quiz. For you to supply: 7 commas—1 comma *if* clause, 1 comma *as* clause, 4 commas parenthetical, 1 comma introductory; 1 semicolon no conjunction; 2 missing words.

490.

(150)

▶ **Warmup.** Your warmup phrase letter is No. 467 on page 367. Copy the last paragraph of this letter as rapidly as you can and as often as time permits.

491. Word Beginnings and Endings

-ment

Electr-

In-

Ul

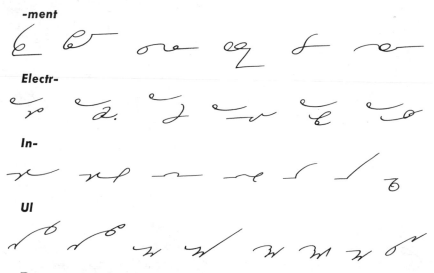

Basement, appointment, agreement, arrangement, payment, garment.
Electricity, electric wiring, electric fan, electric motor, electric razor, electric light.
Install, installation, income, increase, intend, indeed, inside.
Ultimate, ultimately, result, resulted, consult, consultation, insult, adult.

Reading and Writing Practice

492. Transcription Word Study

quarterly Four times a year.

hot-air heat Heat supplied by a furnace that warms the air and sends it direct to each room by means of pipes.

flat charge A fixed, unvarying sum to be paid no matter how much or how little service is rendered.

493.
, conjunction
suitable

hot-air

hyphenated
before noun
, apposition

bear
; no conjunction

(116)

494.
, as clause
electricity

tomorrow's
, if clause

, introductory
wiring

(128)

495.

, introductory
; no conjunction

, introductory
, parenthetical

, introductory
Transcribe:
  $6

necessary
, when clause

annual
, introductory

385

(140)

496.

purchase
, if clause

Transcribe:
   $150
, parenthetical

weekly
, series
; because of comma

special
, apposition

(133)

Personal-Use Check List

Do you substitute shorthand for longhand wherever possible when you

1. Take down your daily assignments?

2. Correspond with friends who know shorthand?

3. Draft compositions and reports?

4. Make entries in your diary?

5. Make notes to yourself on things to do, people to see, appointments to keep, etc.?

Transcription Quiz. For you to supply: 5 commas—2 commas series, 2 commas parenthetical, 1 comma as clause; 1 semicolon no conjunction; 2 missing words.

497.

[shorthand outlines]

(140)

LESSON
70

▶ **Warmup.** For the final time, your warmup letter is No. 467 on page 367. In your best shorthand, write as much of the letter as time permits.

498. Vocabulary Builder

Ū

[shorthand outlines]

Ĭa, Ea

[shorthand outlines]

Īa

[shorthand outlines]

Nd

[shorthand outlines]

Unit, beauty, beautify, unique, human, few, view, review.
Appreciate, appreciated, associate, associated, piano, area, create, miniature.
Appliance, diamond, trial, dial, prior, riot.
Second, cleaned, trained, signed, find, planned, explained.

Reading and Writing Practice

499. Transcription Word Study

   converted   Changed from one form to another.

natural gas   Gas that comes from the earth, as distinguished from gas that is manufactured from coal, etc.

oriental rugs   High-quality rugs made by hand in such eastern countries as Iran, Turkey, etc.

500.

, as clause
area
, apposition

adjustment
, parenthetical

, if clause
converted
arrangements

, parenthetical
; no conjunction
properly

(155)

501.

oriental
, conjunction

, parenthetical
difference

variety
, series

well-trained
   hyphenated
   before noun

, when clause
. courteous
   request

(121)

502.

beautify
, conjunction

hand-cleaning
   hyphenated
   before noun

convenience
repairing

(134)

503.

sleeping
, apposition

, conjunction

; no conjunction
, introductory
weighs

, if clause
further

(118)

All dictators at one time or another during dictation will pause to think of a word, to check some data, or to answer the telephone. When those pauses occur, the wise stenographer, like Julia in the following story, uses the time to good advantage.

504. Don't Waste the Pauses

(shorthand notation)

(257)

Check List

1. When Mr. Davis stopped to think during his dictation, what could Julia have done?

2. What did she actually do?

3. What beneficial effect did her "patching" of her notes have on her rate of transcription?

CHAPTER FIFTEEN

Travel

The last decade has seen the almost unbelievable growth of the airplane — planes that fly faster than sound, planes that carry sixty people nonstop from coast to coast in a matter of hours, planes that take off and land on roof tops — with more wonderful things to come.

In our enthusiasm over the progress of aviation, however, we are sometimes apt to overlook the important role that other forms of transportation play in our everyday economic and social life and the great advances that they also have made in the last decade.

Take the railroads. Each year the railroads transport millions of passengers millions of miles, and they do it with safety and speed. What is more, they provide sleeping and dining accommodations that compare favorably with those of some of the finest hotels.

Take the bus lines. The modern bus has reclining seats in which a person can, if he wishes, sleep in comfort. The modern bus is air conditioned, so that the passengers are comfortable in all kinds of weather. Because bus transportation is inexpensive, many people prefer it to other forms of transportation.

Take the steamship lines. There is nothing more conducive to relaxation and recreation than an ocean voyage. Thousands upon thousands of people travel abroad each year for their vacations, and it is not unusual to hear someone say that the ocean trip was the best part of his vacation. This is easy to understand, because most of the ocean liners are really luxurious floating hotels, with swimming pools, movie theaters, playrooms, etc.

The letters in this chapter deal with railroad, bus, and steamship travel. Perhaps, after you have practiced on these letters, you, too, will have an urge to travel!

505. Phrase Builder. The following list contains 16 phrases. Can you read the list in half a minute?

Miscellaneous Phrases

Of course, of course it is, your order, your orders, we have your order, we hope that, we hope that this, we hope you will, I hope, I hope that, I hope that the, I hope you will, to me, to know, to make, to him.

▶ **Warmup Phrase Letter.** The following 123-word letter, which is your warmup for this chapter, contains 28 phrases. How fast can you read and copy the entire letter?

506.

395

[shorthand outline] **(123)**

Reading and Writing Practice

507. Transcription Word Study

> **booked solid** All accommodations have been reserved.
>
> **memorable** Worthy of being remembered or noted.
>
> **transatlantic** Crossing the Atlantic Ocean.

508.

, parenthetical
, series
scenery.

, as clause
; no conjunction
Wyoming

London's
theaters

396

two-week
    hyphenated
    before noun
, conjunction

, when clause
, apposition
Traveling
509.

(155)

, as clause
New Orleans

15.

; no conjunction
experience

25

, if clause
special

(121)

510.

, if clause
urge

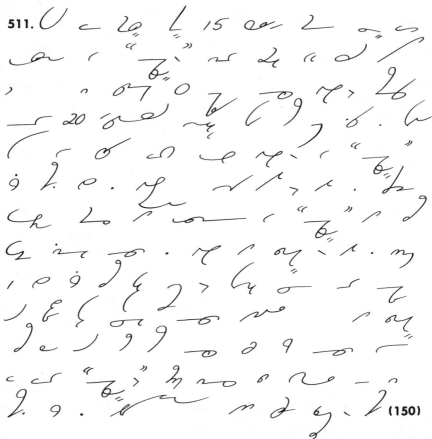

, *if* clause

; no conjunction

(65)

Transcription Quiz. For you to supply: 7 commas—3 commas apposition, 1 comma conjunction, 1 comma introductory, 2 commas *if* clause; 1 semicolon because of comma; 2 missing words.

511.

(150)

Occasionally, a dictator will say a word or a phrase and then change it. Upon reflection, however, he decides that the original word or phrase is better. The dictator might say:

> The accommodations are excellent — no, good; oh, leave it *excellent*.

The best way to handle this situation is to rewrite the restored word or phrase as though it were a completely new form. The stenographer writes the word *excellent*. He then strikes it out and substitutes *good*. Finally, he strikes out *good* and rewrites *excellent*.

Do not try to indicate that the original outline for *excellent* is to be restored; this effort may make your notes difficult to read, with the result that you might not be able to transcribe them correctly.

512. Illustration of Office-Style Dictation

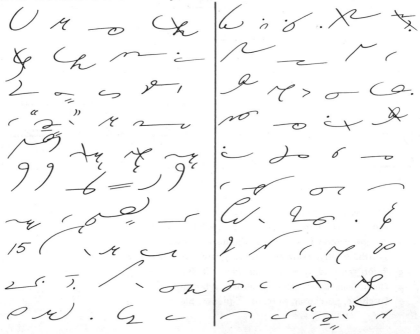

LESSON 72

▶ **Warmup.** Your warmup letter is No. 506 on page 395. Practice the first paragraph, writing it as rapidly as you can and as many times as you can in the time available.

513. Brief-Form Chart. The following chart contains 42 brief forms and derivatives. You should have no difficulty reading it in 30 seconds or less.

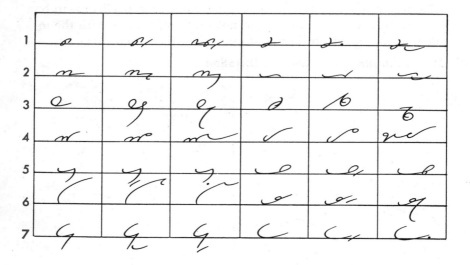

1. Use, used, unused; send, sending, sender.
2. Wonder, wonders, wonderful; work, worked, worker.
3. Where, wherever, whereby; side, decide, inside.
4. Worth, worthy, worthless; ordinary, ordinarily, extraordinary.
5. Refer, referred, referring; like, liked, likely.
6. Time, times, timer; return, returned, returnable.
7. Purchase, purchaser, purchased; please, pleased, pleasing.

514. Geographical Expressions

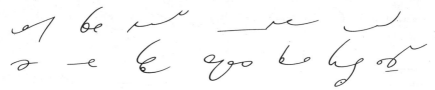

Rio de Janeiro, Buenos Aires, Toronto, Montreal, London.
Canada, Mexico, Brazil, Argentina, Chile, Bolivia, Ecuador.

Reading and Writing Practice

515. Transcription Word Study

round-trip ticket A ticket that entitles a passenger to
ride to his destination and return. A round-trip ticket
usually costs less than two one-way tickets.

travel abroad Travel outside the United States, usually
in European countries.

itinerary A plan of a trip, showing route, stops, length
of stay, etc.

516.

, apposition
round-trip
   hyphenated
   before noun

Montreal
, conjunction

, introductory
immediately

enough
, parenthetical

, introductory
Transcribe:
    $18

(130)

517.

pleasant
, parenthetical
, series

, if clause
; no conjunction

(106)

518.

Rio de Janeiro
, series

, introductory
up-to-the-minute
    hyphenated
    before noun

; because of comma
, series
airplanes

631   16

, if clause
, series

(117)

519.

abroad
, if clause

, when clause
; no conjunction
itinerary

, series
Argentina

(121)

520.

(shorthand outlines)

(70)

Transcription Quiz. For you to supply: 7 commas—2 commas apposition, 1 comma introductory, 1 comma conjunction, 1 comma *if* clause, 2 commas parenthetical; 1 semicolon no conjunction; 2 missing words.

521.

(shorthand outlines)

(121)

▶ **Warmup.** Your warmup phrase letter is No. 506 on page 395. Copy the second paragraph as rapidly as you can and as often as you can in the time available.

522. Word Families

Past Tense, Disjoined

Past Tense, Joined (D)

Past Tense, Joined (T)

Past Tense, (Md)

Used, interested, enclosed, delivered, published, required, returned, corresponded.
Played, received, weighed, maintained, saved, studied, issued.
Helped, increased, decreased, pressed, missed, guessed, traced.
Named, tamed, blamed, seemed, trimmed, dimmed, dreamed.

Reading and Writing Practice

523. Transcription Word Study

   generator A mechanical device that produces electrical energy.

diesel engine An engine that operates with great efficiency with inexpensive fuel, invented by Rudolf Diesel.

524.

recently
, apposition

passenger
, conjunction

, introductory
diesel-powered
hyphenated
before noun

; because of comma
, series
experimentation

, if clause

(151)

525.
world's
major
atomic

, conjunction
freight
area

196

, introductory
successfully

, parenthetical
equipment
machinery

, if clause
; no conjunction
center

(177)

526.
, introductory
crowds

(141)

movement
teamwork

, when clause
; no conjunction

527.

25

1933   10

1940

12   29

29

, introductory   250

70

safely
comfortably

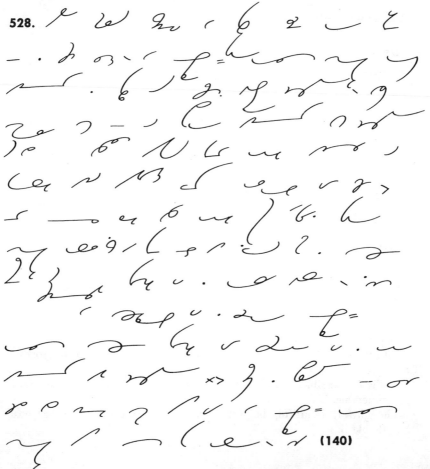

(135)

Transcription Quiz. For you to supply: 4 commas—1 comma as clause, 1 comma conjunction, 1 comma introductory, 1 comma *if* clause; 1 semicolon no conjunction; 2 missing words.

528.

(140)

LESSON 74

▶ **Warmup.** Your warmup letter is No. 506 on page 395. Copy the third paragraph of the letter as rapidly as you can and as many times as you can in the time available.

529. Word Beginnings and Endings

De-

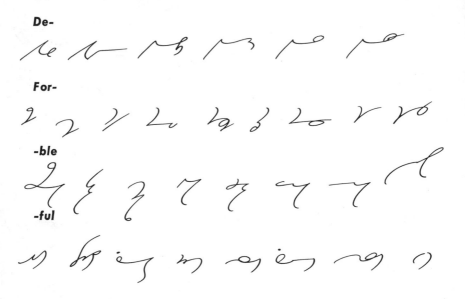

For-

-ble

-ful

Depress, department, delicious, de luxe, delay, delight.

Effort, comfort, forward, foremost, forecast, foresee, foreman, fortune, fortunate.

Available, possible, comfortably, trouble, sensible, honorable, marketable, timetable.

Thoughtful, beautiful, helpful, successful, careful, harmful, grateful, thankful.

Reading and Writing Practice

530. Transcription Word Study

depressing (*verb*) Pushing or pressing down.

simplifying Making it easy to understand or operate.

resort (*noun*) A vacation area; usually where groups of people gather.

531.

, conjunction
appreciate

, parenthetical

15465

, when clause
successful

suggestions
, if clause

(149)

532.

411

; no conjunction
, introductory
durable

, introductory
baggage
children

, as clause
equipped

(141)

533.

expenditure
, series

; because of comma
simplifying

, when clause
worth-while

**hyphenated
before noun**

whether
, introductory

discuss
, apposition

(154)

534.

, introductory
de luxe
; no conjunction

(90)

535.

, series

, when clause
St. Louis

aboard
, conjunction

(74)

Transcription Quiz. For you to supply: 6 commas—1 comma as clause, 1 comma introductory, 1 comma conjunction, 1 comma *if* clause, 2 commas parenthetical; 1 semicolon because of comma; 2 missing words.

536.

(120)

▶ **Warmup.** Your warmup letter is No. 506 on page 395. Copy the entire letter as rapidly as you can. If time permits, copy it a second time, in your best shorthand.

537. Vocabulary Builder

Th

Omission of Ow

Omission of Short U

Tern, Term, Dern

Three, thread, thrill, though, both, thick, teeth, thin.
Brown, found, round, sound, town, down, drown, frown.
Touch, jump, front, come, judge, smudge, lunch.
Turn, turned, term, termed, determine, determination, modern.

Reading and Writing Practice

538. Transcription Word Study

    rack The shelf above a seat in a bus, plane, or train on which to place wraps and packages.

reclining chairs. Chairs that can be tilted backward for greater comfort.

Pullman A railroad passenger car equipped with luxurious and comfortable furnishings, for which an extra charge is made.

539.

, apposition
Pittsburgh

1:30
gray
, when clause
; because of comma

, introductory
, apposition
sewn
awe

, introductory
; no conjunction
gloves

(106)

, if clause
. courteous
   request

540.
, introductory
, parenthetical
planning

, introductory
, series
temperature

reclining

, when clause
economical

(109)

541.

, when clause
round trip
   no noun,
   no hyphen

25,

②

round-trip
   hyphenated
   before noun

③

50,

(122)

Secretarial Pointer

The most productive worker is not always the fastest worker. The slower, but efficient, worker may turn out as much work as the faster worker—even more, perhaps—because he keeps his waste motions to a minimum. The ideal worker, of course, is the one who is both rapid and efficient.

In the story that follows, you will learn why Betty out-produced Ruth, even though Ruth was the better typist and transcriber.

542. It Pays to Organize

(250)

Check List

1. Why did Betty turn out more work than Ruth turned out, even though Ruth could write and transcribe shorthand faster?

2. Where did Betty keep her eraser? Where did Ruth keep hers?

3. When did Betty proofread her letters? When did Ruth proofread hers?

CHAPTER SIXTEEN

Radio and Television

"I don't believe it; there ain't no such animal," said the farmer when he saw the giraffe. If our great grandfathers had heard a modern radio bring them a concert by a symphony orchestra that was playing hundreds of miles away, they, too, would have said, "I don't believe it; there isn't (our great grandfathers wouldn't have said *ain't!*) any such animal." If they had sat before one of today's television sets and had had a bird's-eye view of every play of a ball game that was being played in some other city, they would have been convinced that they were dreaming!

But today a radio is as much a part of the furnishings of every household as the kitchen stove or electric lights. In fact, in many households, each member of the family has his own radio.

The television is not far behind. The day is rapidly passing when all the neighbors gather in the home of the one family on the street that has television — more and more families are getting their own sets.

Radio and television have had a profound effect on our everyday living and have done much to enrich our lives. They have brought within easy reach of everyone not only the finest in entertainment but also many educational opportunities.

If you have ambitions to make radio and television your lifework, there is no better way to get a foothold in those industries than through shorthand and typewriting.

The letters in this chapter are typical of those that would pass over your desk if you were a stenographer or secretary to an executive in the radio or television industry.

543. Phrase Builder. The following list contains 29 phrases. Because you have seen these phrases many times, you should be able to read the entire list easily in 30 seconds.

Omission of Words

Words Modified

Understand, Understood

Able

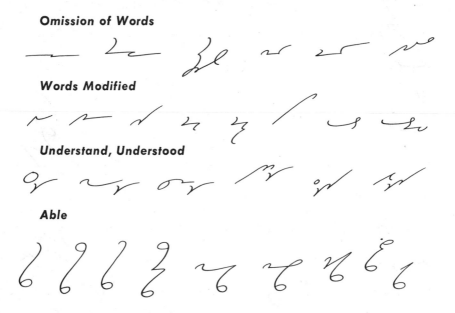

More and more, for a moment, for a few days, one of the, some of them, two or three.

To our, to him, your order, as soon as, as soon as possible, to do, let us, let us know.

I understand, you will understand, I cannot understand, do you understand, he understood, it is understood.

Have been able, I have been able, you have been able, I have not been able, you will be able, you may be able, you should be able, has been able, to be able.

▶ **Warmup Phrase Letter.** Your warmup phrase letter for this chapter contains 157 words. There are 29 phrases in this letter. How fast can you read and copy the entire letter?

544.

[shorthand outlines] (157)

Reading and Writing Practice

545. Transcription Word Study

warrant (verb) To justify, to authorize.

radio-phonograph A combination radio and turntable unit that receives radio programs and through which phonograph records may be played, using the same amplifier and speaker.

ascertain To find out, determine.

546. *[shorthand outline]*

, apposition
, as clause
; because of comma

, apposition
, if clause
immediately

; because of comma
, introductory
radio

(122)

547. *[shorthand outline]*

sole

piece
; no conjunction

, **parenthetical**
; **no conjunction**
budget

, **parenthetical**
convenience

trade-in
  hyphenated
  before noun
, **series**

(155)

548.

Nash's
, **introductory**

worth-while
  hyphenated
  before noun
, *when clause*

often
audience
, **introductory**

ascertain
listening
, **conjunction**

(132)

Transcription Quiz. For you to supply: 5 commas—1 comma as clause, 1 comma introductory, 2 commas parenthetical, 1 comma *if* clause; 1 semicolon no conjunction; 2 missing words.

549. *[shorthand outlines]* **(161)**

A businessman may occasionally decide to transpose words or phrases for emphasis or some other reason. The simplest way to indicate the transposition of a word or phrase is to use the regular printer's sign for transposition.

The dictator might say:

> The radio is the least expensive and most effective advertising medium for our products — make that *most effective* and *least expensive*.

In your shorthand, you would make the change in this way:

You would then be careful, when you transcribe, to type the word *and* after the word *effective*.

550. Illustration of Office-Style Dictation

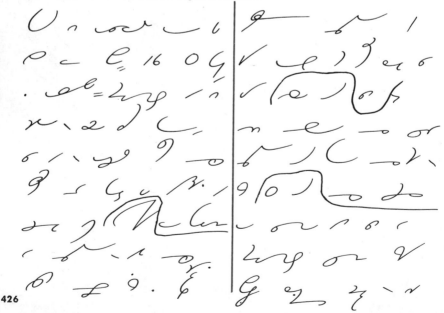

▶ **Warmup.** Your warmup phrase letter is No. 544 on page 422. Write the first paragraph as rapidly and as often as you can in the time you have available.

551. Brief-Form Chart. The following chart contains 42 brief forms and derivatives. Can you read the chart in 30 seconds or less?

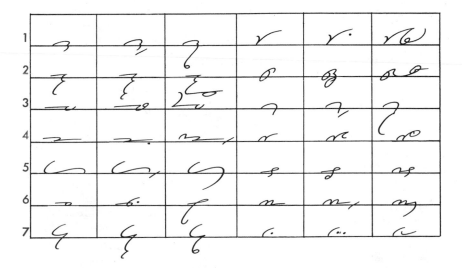

1. Consider, considered, considerably; stand, standing, standpoint.
2. Newspaper, newspapers, newspaperman; out, outside, outline.
3. Most, mostly, foremost; question, questioned, questionable.
4. Number, numbering, unnumbered; other, others, otherwise.
5. Progress, progressed, progressive; necessary, necessarily, unnecessary.
6. Any, anything, anybody; wonder, wondered, wonderful.
7. Purpose, purposes, purposely; thing-think, thinking, thinker.

552. Geographical Expressions

Denver, Louisville, Miami, Newark, Minneapolis, Houston.
Colorado, Kentucky, Florida, Georgia, North Carolina, South Carolina,
Virginia, West Virginia.

Reading and Writing Practice

553. Transcription Word Study

supplement (verb) Add to.

cuts (noun) Engraved blocks or plates for printing.

telecast (verb) To broadcast by television.

554.

two-page
four-color
hyphenated
before noun

, as clause
; because of comma

, parenthetical
supplement
local

material
, apposition

standpoint
, conjunction

555.

Louisville
Company's
, introductory

, parenthetical
installed

, series
courteously
skillfully

; no conjunction
post card

(125)

556.

, introductory
, series
musicals

, parenthetical
however

recommended
thousands

time-payment
hyphenated
before noun

, if clause

, when clause
quality

(190)

557.

20-inch
hyphenated
before noun

Transcribe:
$500
, conjunction

, when clause *[shorthand]*

, if clause *[shorthand]*

[shorthand] **(131)**

Transcription Quiz. For you to supply: 7 commas—1 comma conjunction, 1 comma introductory, 4 commas parenthetical, 1 comma *if* clause; 1 semicolon because of comma; 2 missing words.

558. *[shorthand]*

[shorthand] **(158)**

LESSON 78

▶ **Warmup.** Your warmup letter for this lesson is No. 544 on page 422. Write the second paragraph of the letter as rapidly as you can and as often as you can in the time you have available.

559. Word Families

Tele-

-cast

-titute, -titution

-work

Television, telephone, telescope, telegram, Teletype.
Cast, telecast, broadcast, downcast, overcast, forecast, recast.
Substitute, constitute, institute, destitute; substitution, constitution, institution.
Work, network, groundwork, framework, homework, teamwork.

Reading and Writing Practice

560. Transcription Word Study

marine Pertaining to water; usually the sea or ocean.

in conjunction   Along with or happening at the same time.

rehearsal   Reciting, going through, or repeating over and over.

561. *(shorthand)*

, introductory
permission

(shorthand)

studio
currently

(shorthand)

, parenthetical
source
receive

(shorthand)

, if clause
publicity

(151)

562.
originally
, introductory
; because of comma

(shorthand)

, introductory
, series
level

chimneys
delicate

exploration

endure
wrecks
, introductory

worth-while
  hyphenated
  before noun

(187)

563.

, as clause
usually

, if clause

TV

24

viewer's
convenience
mind

, if clause
repairs

; no conjunction

(146)

564.

believe
, as clause
, apposition

, parenthetical
rehearsals

, conjunction
roles
scripts

[shorthand outlines]

cameras
, conjunction

(155)

Transcription Quiz. For you to supply: 8 commas—2 commas when clause, 1 comma as clause, 2 commas if clause, 1 comma introductory, 2 commas parenthetical; 1 semicolon because of comma; 2 missing words.

565. *[shorthand outlines]*

(146)

▶ **Warmup.** Your warmup letter is No. 544 on page 422. Write the third paragraph of the letter as rapidly as you can and as many times as you can in the time available.

566. Word Beginnings and Endings

-gram

-ment

En-, In-

Inter-, Enter-

Program, programs, monogram, diagram, radiogram.

Appointment, department, basement, employment, measurement, statement.

Enjoy, encourage, engrave, enforce; invite, information, increase, intense.

Entering, entered, enterprise, entertainment; interest, interestingly, interfere, international.

Reading and Writing Practice

567. Transcription Word Study

    flair Special aptitude.

audition A hearing, particularly to determine a speaker's or a musical performer's ability.

prearrange Plan beforehand.

"live" program A program that is telecast as it is being performed; a program not previously recorded on film.

568.

auditioning
, conjunction

, when clause
college
scholarship

, introductory
lead
amateur

, if clause
appointment

(132)

569.
originating
studios
audience

, apposition
Transcribe:
June 10

; because of comma
, introductory

prearranged
, if clause

, if clause

(132)

570.

network's
worth-while
hyphenated
before noun

, as clause
receive
daily

contestants
, parenthetical
; no conjunction

, *if clause*

opportunity
; *no conjunction*　(151)

571.
, *conjunction*
, *introductory*
consequently

announcing
, *conjunction*

, *introductory*
; *because of comma*
flair

, *when clause*

, *if clause*
recommend

(129)

572.

, *apposition*
Transcribe:
　October 9

440

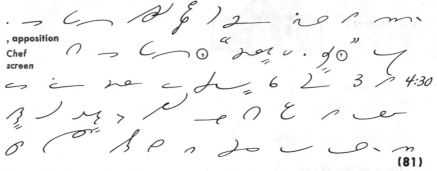

, apposition
Chef
screen

(81)

Transcription Quiz. For you to supply: 5 commas—2 commas introductory, 2 commas series, 1 comma as clause; 2 semicolons because of
comma; 2 missing words.

573.

(140)

LESSON 80

▶ **Warmup.** This will be your final warmup on letter No. 544, page 422. Make one copy of the letter in your best shorthand.

574. Vocabulary Builder

Days of the Week

Months of the Year

Omission of T

X

Tuesday, Friday, Sunday, Monday, Saturday, Thursday, Wednesday.
February, July, January, August, June, December, November, April,
    September, October.
Act, actor, effect, conduct, deduct, fact, expect, intact.
Tax, taxes, relax, fix, mix, complex, reflex.

Reading and Writing Practice

575. Transcription Word Study

    sketch (*noun*) A rough description or outline.

    absorbed in Wholly engaged in; fully occupied by.

576.

, apposition

Transcribe: 7:30

  April 16

income-tax

  hyphenated
  before noun

unfortunately

, introductory

; because of comma

, parenthetical

whether

transcript

, parenthetical

; no conjunction

(123)

577.

, as clause

, apposition

, parenthetical

President's

443

, apposition
; because of comma
, if clause
approval

substitution
, if clause
initial

578.

kdda

, introductory
sketch

, series
, parenthetical
humorous

popular
, conjunction

well-known
  hyphenated
  before noun

(153)

(136)

When businessmen dictate, they sometimes become so engrossed in the subject matter of their dictation that they unconsciously use a wrong word or choose an incorrect verb or fail to complete a sentence. They do not worry about these errors, however, because they know that their stenographers, if they are worth their salt, will correct them. Katherine, in the following story, unfortunately was not worth her salt!

579. "But That's What You Said"

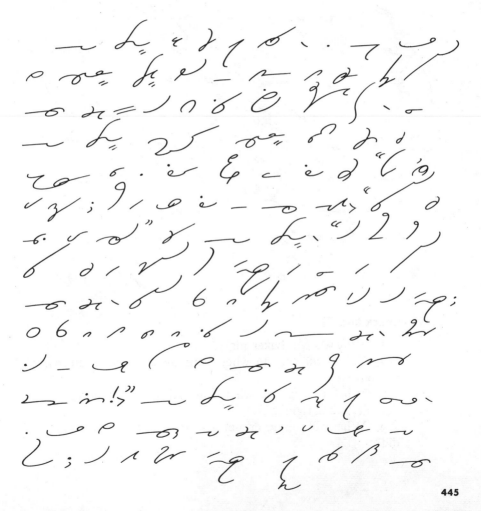

(280)

Check List

1. Why was Mr. Baker angry?
2. What will you do when your dictator makes an obvious error?
3. What will you do when something in your notes doesn't "sound right"?
4. What will you never, never do that Katherine Bates did?

BRIEF FORMS IN ALPHABETIC ORDER

	A	B	C	D	E	F
1						
2						
3						
4						
5						
6						
7						
8						
9						
10						
11						
12						
13						
14						
15						
16						
17						
18						

	A	B	C	D	E	F
19						
20						
21						
22						
23						
24						
25						
26						
27						
28						
29						
30						
31						